Praise for *An End to Arguing*

"In this very useful book, Charlie and Linda Bloom have an assembly of tools for every occasion. Every couple should keep it beside their bed and absorb it until they internalize it all."

—**Harville Hendrix,** PhD, and **Helen LaKelly Hunt**, PhD, authors of *Getting the Love You Want: A Guide for Couples and Making Marriage Simple*

"Every couple fights and struggles. Successful couples know how to fight right and repair conflict. Linda and Charlie Bloom are two of the world's best guides through the land mines of love and commitment. *An End Arguing* is a handbook to a deeper love and a richer life together."

—**Doug Abrams,** co-author of *The Book of Joy* and *The Book of Hope*

"Linda and Charlie Bloom really know relationship dynamics inside and out, and it shows—and glows—on every page. This is a beautifully levelheaded guide to managing the conflicts that love inevitably flushes up to the surface and is full of the Blooms' relentless faith in people's ability to navigate them gracefully, and effectively. They make a compelling case for the radical idea that conflict is optional and not inevitable in relationships. Readers are sure to benefit from the heartfulness and thoroughness of this book's explorations."

—**Gregg Levoy,** author of *Callings: Finding and Following an Authentic Life*, and *Vital Signs: The Nature and Nurture of Passion*

"This book could be titled, *Everything You've Ever Wanted to Know About Conflict.* It contains pretty much all the best practices and best ideas anyone interested in this topic will ever need to know. And it's not just for couples. There is wisdom in these pages for parents, teachers, friendships, business relationships, as well as for groups and teams."

—**Susan Campbell,** PhD, author of *The Couples Journey,*
Getting Real, and *Five-Minute Relationship Repair*

"In our forty years working with couples, the inability to resolve conflict is one of the top reasons couples don't make it. If you're willing to roll up your sleeves and do some very important work, read this book carefully. It will save your marriage! It will be your go-to manual for healthy conflict resolution."

—**Barry Vissell,** MD, and **Joyce Vissell**, RN, MS,
authors of *The Shared Heart*

"Linda and Charlie Bloom give remarkably thorough coverage of how to transform conflict around differences that results in painful estrangement into mutual and self-appreciation, and emotional closeness. Throughout the book are tools for connecting positively and stories that show just how many couples have replaced blaming and shaming with open-heartedness, vulnerability, and honesty."

—**Marcia Naomi Berger**, LCSW, author of *Marriage
Meetings for Lasting Love: 30 Minutes a Week to the
Relationship You've Always Wanted*

"Linda and Charlie Bloom's latest book, *An End to Arguing* is filled with 101 reader-friendly, practical nuggets of guidance and wisdom that will come in handy to anyone who has ever felt the need for a manual for managing and preventing conflict, not only in personal relationships, but in any relationship in which differences arise. Having been married for fifty years, and having practiced relationship counseling for over forty of those years, the Blooms have paid their dues in the trenches of committed partnership and have brought the collective wisdom of their experiences into a book that not only promotes an acceptance of the inevitable differences that are contained in all relationships, but an appreciation for them. These two have truly walked their talk and the evidence is illuminated on every page!"

—**Ken Dychtwald,** author of *Bodymind*; and **Maddy Dychtwald**, author of *Cycles: How We Live, Work and Buy*

"*An End to Arguing* puts the Blooms into the pantheon with the Gottmans' and Hendrixs'—a must read for anyone who wants to unearth the usual dysfunctionality of marriage and transform it into calm, compassionate conversations."

—**Ira Israel,** author of *How to Survive Your Childhood Now that You're an Adult*

"*An End to Arguing* is the ultimate handbook of conflict management, resolution, and avoidance that you will ever need. Charlie and Linda's book provides excellent guidance to anyone who has ever felt the pain and hopelessness that unreconciled differences can generate within intimate relationships. Their book offers hope where there had been despair, and a return to deep love, when we've lost our way."

—**Sage Lavine,** author of *Women Rocking Business*

"The Blooms have written another book that knocks it out of the park. Packed with clear, concise, and hard-earned wisdom, each page allows us to reflect on our relationships so that they might offer us more richness, depth, and delight."

—**John Amodeo,** PhD, author of *Dancing with Fire: A Mindful Way to Loving Relationships*

"This book is jam-packed with insights into what keeps fights from getting out of hand and makes them productive. The Blooms share hard-earned wisdom, in a very simple form, about what really works."

—**James Creighton,** author of *Loving Through Your Differences*

"What I especially appreciate about this book is the authors' authenticity and compassion that shines through every page. They are clearly committed to helping to reduce suffering and create a more compassionate world by helping readers to understand themselves and others, and to learn how to actualize their desire for intimacy and connection I also appreciate the quality of the writing, which I find clear and easy to follow (a rarity!) and, of course, the wisdom they share."

—**Melanie Joy,** PhD, author of *Getting Relationship Right*

"This is a marvelous book written by two highly experienced, expert couples' therapists. Filed with fascinating examples from their practices and tons of helpful insights and suggestions, it's a must-read for any couple, married or not, who want to learn about or improve their relationship."

—**John W. Jacobs,** MD, author of *All You Need Is Love and Other Lies About Marriage*

"There are bushels of relationship advice books. What distinguishes those by Linda and Charlie Bloom, including their latest *An End to Arguing* is their fusion of their wisdom and personal transparency. Their own story humanizes and makes credible their abundant advice. This well-written compassionate book is worth any couple's time."

—**David Kerns,** author of *Fortnight on Maxwell Street* and *Standard of Care*

"The Blooms latest book, *An End Arguing*, is a most thorough and masterful examination of relational conflict, is written with simplicity and a refreshing absence of psychological jargon and theory. One recognizes throughout these pages, the hard-won truths that could only emerge from a couple who has taken their own relationship seriously enough to give it their deepest focus and energy with persistence over the decades. Couples will find this book a consummate reference manual if they want to avoid many of the painful detours on the way to a ripe and satisfying union."

—Don Rosenthal, co-author of *Learning to Love*

"Linda and Charlie Bloom's latest installment of lessons learned from their professional counseling and life experiences presents practical advice and useful insights that will benefit every reader. In *An End Arguing*, they provide a compendium of tools, tactics, and techniques that offer ways to manage challenges, and reveal perspectives that enhance relationships. Their book is certain to guide readers toward more fulfilling, sustainable, and enriching relationships."

—Brad Kane, author of *Pitchfork Populism*

"A simple, elegant playbook for bringing your best, most loving and humble self to the people and relationships you treasure."

—Ken Druck, PhD, author of *Courageous Aging*

"Linda and Charlie have made an end to arguing accessible, mind opening, and oh-so-relevant in our fragmented, Humpty Dumpty world."

—Dawna Markova, PhD, author of *Collaborative Intelligence: Thinking with People Who Think Differently*

"Years of helping couples overcome their difficulties have given Linda and Charlie Bloom a vast store of knowledge about how to deal with conflict successfully. That knowledge is distilled in this wonderful book, which I recommend without reservation. Written in a vivid and accessible manner, this book can be mined over and over for its nuggets of wisdom."

—**Lewis Engel,** PhD, author with Tom Ferguson, MD, of
*Imaginary Crimes: Why You Punish Yourself and
How to Stop*

"Charlie and Linda's latest book, *An End to Arguing* is brimming with insights, strategies, soulful counsel and deep wisdom. It gives hope and inspiration to everyone,—whether you're in a new relationship or have been together for over for fifty years, as they have!"

—**Renee Trudeau,** author of *The Mother's Guide to
Self-Renewal*

"In their latest book, Linda and Charlie Bloom break down common stumbling blocks like conflict avoidance, the pursuer/distancer pattern and the impact of unfinished business, to help you not only fight fair, but grow together through your differences. There is valuable information on literally every page. This book is destined to become a well-thumbed reference on your bedroom bookshelf."

—**Tina Gilbertson,** author of *Reconnecting with
Your Estranged Adult Child*

"Linda and Charlie Bloom have created your permanent conflict guidebook. Every page contains gems of wisdom to help you navigate the terrain of inevitable clashes. Why stay in pain? Instead let Charlie and Linda light your way."

—**Ellyn Bader,** PhD, author of *Tell Me No Lies: How to Face
the Truth and Build a Loving Marriage*

"Imagine walking through a minefield in the dark. Now turn the lights on. Linda and Charlie flip the switch with 101 mines that you will want to see before you start walking. I loved this book. It offers practical tools and real-world insights to nurture and support lasting and meaningful relationships. Linda and Charlie have created a Bible with 101 commandments. Break them and you will suffer the wrath. Follow them and you will see experience heaven on earth."

—**Andy Chaleff,** author of *The Last Letter* and *The Wounded Healer*

"*An End to Arguing* is an amazingly comprehensive presentation of relational challenges in which the commitment to non-hostility is the prelude to fruitful negotiations. Perhaps the universal first instruction to couples in distress could be: 'Stop! Calm down! Get a grip! Now talk.'"

—**Sylvia Boorstein,** PhD, co-founder of the Spirit Rock Meditation Center, author of *Happiness is an Inside Job: Practicing for a Joyful Life*

"Powerful medicine is offered here: a book that expands your understanding, supports, kindly instructs, and skillfully challenges you to grow in love, and shows you 101 wise and helpful ways to do it!"

—**Jack Kornfield,** PhD, author of *A Path with Heart*

"The Blooms' latest book, *An End to Arguing* not only lives up to the promise of its title but it provides valuable guidance to navigate through the inevitable differences that occur not only in committed partnerships, but in relationships of all kinds. If you've ever wished for a manual that will help you to prevent painful interpersonal conflict and effectively repair it if it does occur, this is the book you've been waiting for!"

—**Margaret Paul,** author of *Inner Bonding*

An End to Arguing: 101 Valuable Lessons for All Relationships

by Linda and Charlie Bloom

© Copyright 2022 Linda and Charlie Bloom

ISBN 978-1-64663-810-9

Published by

 köehlerbooks™

3705 Shore Drive
Virginia Beach, VA 23455
800-435-4811
www.koehlerbooks.com

AN
END TO
ARGUING

101 Valuable Lessons for
All Relationships

LINDA AND CHARLIE BLOOM

Authors of the best-selling book *101 Things I Wish I Knew When I Got Married*

VIRGINIA BEACH
CAPE CHARLES

Other Books by Linda and Charlie Bloom

101 Things I Wish I Knew When I Got Married: Simple Lessons to Make Love Last

Secrets of Great Marriages: Real Truths from Real Couples about Lasting Love

Happily Ever After . . . and 39 Other Myths about Love

That Which Doesn't Kill Us: How One Couple Became Stronger at the Broken Places

This book is dedicated to our children, Jesse, Sarah, and Eben, and our grandchildren, Devin, Ashton, and Seth, with gratitude to them and all they have given to us and taught us.

Table of Contents

Introduction 1

1. Yes, it really is possible to avoid arguments. 7

2. Practice does not necessarily make perfect, but it sure helps. 10

3. From breakdown to breakthrough 13

4. Transforming desire into intention 16

5. To vent or not to vent 19

6. Nonreactive listening 22

7. Adults sometimes need time-outs too. 26

8. The victim 28

9. Are you conflict avoidant? 31

10. Why winning doesn't work 35

11. Negotiation 38

12. Terms of engagement 41

13. Control freaks 44

14. Having a conversation about having a conversation 47

15. When hope isn't enough 49

16. The shortest complete sentence in the English language 52

17. There's two sides to every story 54

18. Extroverts and introverts 58

19. Opposites and complements 62

20. Projection 65

21. Making a molehill out of a mountain 67

22. Are you complete? 69

23. How to finish unfinished business 72

24. Reframing..74

25. The downside of "doing what comes naturally"..............76

26. The ultimate danger sport...78

27. Schismogenesis...81

28. The high cost of winning an argument............................84

29. The real deal about deal-breakers 86

30. Differences are inevitable; conflict is optional................89

31. Preventing differences from turning into conflicts............92

32. Holding the tension of the opposites.............................95

33. Confirmation bias 97

34. Why you shouldn't pick your battles 100

35. Emotional intimacy 103

36. The greatest gift you can give your partner 107

37. Going for the gusto! 109

38. Enlightened self-interest..112

39. The power of vulnerability 115

40. Every accusation is an autobiography...........................118

41. Making room for the shadow 121

42. Who's in your shadow? 123

43. It's not about finding; it's about digging! 125

44. Stuffers and shouters..128

45. Authenticity 131

46. When intrapersonal conflicts become interpersonal 133

47. Are you checking in or checking out? 137

48. Putting an end to "zero-sum thinking".........................139

49. Violence can come in many forms................................142

50. Beware of the dangers of arrogance.............................144

51. Are you fighting or engaging in conscious combat?....................147

52. Transforming your attachment into a preference 150

53. To disclose or not to disclose 153

54. Sometimes it's better to say nothing. 155

55. Competing commitments 157

56. Boundaries: where do you draw the line? 160

57. Manipulation: The costs outweigh the benefits..........................163

58. Mind over matter 167

59. Family rules and family roles..170

60. The biggest relationship threat 173

61. Triggered? Try this. 175

62. Irreconcilable differences 177

63. Don't use these three words. 180

64. Can I give you some feedback?...183

65. From fear to fearlessness 186

66. Primum non nocere...188

67. The hidden cost of people pleasing..190

68. Me or we? 193

69. Flooding 196

70. From avoidance to engagement..198

71. Sore spots..200

72. If you don't want her to be a nag, treat her like a thoroughbred...203

73. Honesty...205

74. When "I'm sorry" just isn't enough..209

75. Forgiveness...211

76. Don't bring out the big guns. 213

77. Confessions of a recovering helper 215

78. Are you talking about money or fighting about it?......................217

79. Don't be a SAP (speculations, assumptions, and projection).....220

80. Ten magic words...223

81. The high cost of nursing a grudge..226

82. Connectors and freedom fighters 230

83. Attachment, nonattachment, and detachment.............................234

84. Safety..237

85. Ragers, bullies, and intimidators..240

86. Who's got the power? 242

87. Agreements 244

88. Grievances 247

89. What we appreciate appreciates. 249

90. Complaints are highly underrated. 252

91. When being wrong is all right 255

92. Damage control 258

93. Thinking about getting marriage counseling?...............................260

94. Constructive criticism generally isn't constructive......................264

95. Sarcasm: sometimes it's not so funny...266

96. Creative synthesis...268

97. Are you a champion of repair? 271

98. Clearing 274

99. When he (or she) won't open up 277

100. It's never too late to have a happy childhood..............................280

101. The payoffs 283

Acknowledgments...286

About the Authors 287

Introduction

Relationships involve two seemingly contradictory forces:
   (1) Common ground
   (2) Different perspectives

The first has to do with shared values, views, and orientations that promote feelings of connection and security. The second has to do with an expansion of one's perception of possibilities that can enrich one's growth and development. It's the awareness of the potential for both security and growth that attracts us to another person. When both of these needs are met, to a degree that is satisfying to both partners, the quality of the relationship is mutually fulfilling. When there is failure to fulfill both sides of the equation, it's a different story. When an imbalance occurs, the relationship becomes at risk of becoming unstable. These are the times that arguments are most likely to occur.

When we use the word *argument*, we are referring to a specific type of interaction between two people in which there is a disagreement wherein each partner's primary intention is to coerce the other to act, feel, speak, or think in ways that they hope will satisfy needs or desires that they are currently experiencing. When both people operate from this intention, it sets up a self-reinforcing cycle that becomes progressively antagonistic and painful and/or threatening. If unchecked, this downward spiral will cause increasing suffering to both parties until an uneasy and usually temporary pause in hostilities occurs. The feelings of hurt, fear, anger, and pain generated in the process don't go away but are submerged in the minds and bodies of the participants until they get reawakened by another similar circumstance. And so it goes.

This pattern is what we refer to when we talk about arguments. And while we can't help but bring different perspectives, preferences, intentions, desires, and points of view to our relationship, we can respond to our differences in ways that don't take us down a slippery slope.

As anyone who has ever experienced the agonies and ecstasies of a committed partnership knows, if you stick with it long enough, you'll get to experience both of these extremes. Heaven knows, we have had our share of both in the over fifty years of blissful and not-so-blissful times we've shared. We are very different in our personalities, but one of the things we have learned over the years is that it's not the similarities but the differences that create our chemistry.

We've observed that this phenomenon seems to hold true for most couples. Given this tendency, it's not surprising that at times relationships can seem at best "challenging" and at worst "impossible." Many of the authors' difficulties have proven to be related to our different perspectives and life histories. Adding to the complexity of our situation is the fact that we were both only twenty-one when our relationship began, and neither of us were raised in families that modeled skillful conflict resolution.

Linda: Although most couples tend to complement each other with their differences, ours have always seemed inordinately extreme. In many ways, we represent opposite ends of the spectrum: I am detailed-oriented; Charlie is a generalist; I favor strict parenting, and Charlie doesn't; I am an outgoing, social person, while Charlie is more of an introvert; I go to bed early, and he likes to stay up late; I like to get to the airport with hours to spare, but a fifteen-minute wait is too much for him; I believe in planning and preparation, where Charlie favors spontaneity; I seek connection when I am stressed; Charlie prefers solitude; when we teach, I use notes; he just wings it. The list goes on, but you get the idea. Las Vegas oddsmakers probably would have given us about a one in a thousand chance to make it to fifty weeks, to say nothing of fifty years!

In the early years of our marriage, neither of us had any idea about how to deal with our differences. We spent a fair amount of time either in conflict or in avoidance of it. It wasn't the differences themselves that kept getting us in trouble but our reactions to them. Like many couples, we attempted to do away with our differences by trying to change each other or ourselves. Homogenizing our personalities, and thus eliminating the sources of conflict, seemed at the time to be a good idea. This strategy, we eventually discovered, doesn't work. Instead, it produced further conflict, both within ourselves and between us.

There was more to our relationship than suffering and struggle, of course. Had there not been, we could not and would not have stayed together. From our earliest days, a deeply loving connection has sustained us through the ordeals, power struggles, and disappointments. We shared experiences as a couple and as a family that were mutually joyous and deeply fulfilling.

But even the strongest bonds are not immune to the toll ongoing struggles can impose. For us, the turning point came when after fifteen years of marriage, conflict and frustration had worn us down, and we both were seriously questioning whether it was worth it to go on together. Despite a strong desire to preserve our marriage and family, the strain of dealing with irreconcilable differences got to be too much.

We could see why couples who love each other choose divorce. For both of us there was sadness and relief in that recognition. We were grief-stricken that we seemed to be about to lose our marriage but simultaneously relieved that the years of struggle might finally be coming to an end.

Fortunately, facing the reality of divorce led us both to realize what we stood to lose and how much we both really wanted to preserve our marriage. We knew there had to be another way, and that awareness helped us make the leap from tolerating our differences to appreciating them.

Attempting to dissolve our differences hadn't worked, so instead we tried to look for the hidden gifts in them. We knew, at least intellectually, that these differences had drawn us together and made us attractive to each other. At the same time, they were the primary triggers of our defensive patterns that inevitably created conflict.

The challenge was to try to change neither ourselves nor each other but rather to honor our own uniqueness while strengthening the bonds of respect between us. Learning to see our differences as the means for becoming more loving, rather than as obstacles to overcome, has profoundly altered how we relate to each other and everyone else in our lives. In our work with couples, we have found that while it does require effort and intentionality to adopt this orientation, it becomes less difficult and more natural once the commitment is made.

The understanding and healing we have experienced has shaped our relationship into the treasure it is now. Coming as close as we did to losing our marriage, we learned to truly care for and appreciate each other to a degree we may not have experienced otherwise. We live with a deep sense of gratitude, and these days we rarely—even briefly—take our relationship for granted.

We are two ordinary people who, through a combination of good help, good luck, hard work, commitment, and a steadfast faith in a shared vision, made it through the ordeals of our marriage and learned to grow from those experiences.

It was because of, not despite, our ordeals that we found the confidence in the power of intention to heal from a wounded past and ultimately become even stronger, both individually and together. One of the great gifts we have received throughout this process has been the opportunity to share with others the wisdom we gained and to help them effectively manage and even avoid the mistakes we have made, as well as to repair those that are unavoidable.

The late spiritual teacher Stephen Levine, co-author of *Embracing the Beloved*, referred to marriage as "the ultimate danger sport." "People can," he said, "learn more about themselves in a week in a relationship than by sitting in a cave, meditating for a year." Having tried both marriage and meditation, we have to agree. The development of self-understanding is both the means to and the gift of marriage—simple but not necessarily easy.

As much as we have grown and thrived in our marriage, we would be the first to admit that marriage is not for everyone. Some people do not feel the desire to choose a long-term, committed partnership and are content to live without one. We honor and support their choice. Others choose not to marry out of a fear that they haven't sufficiently recovered from wounds they experienced in previous relationships, perhaps going back as far as early childhood. They may believe that they are too badly damaged to co-create a healthy relationship. We both strongly challenge that belief.

Others have chosen the path of committed partnership for a variety of reasons, many of which are unconscious but compelling nonetheless. This book includes some of the challenges most couples encounter and was in no way written to present a Pollyanna perspective of relationships. We hope that our attempt to provide realistic rather than idealistic views does not discourage you from exercising your commitment muscle.

Most couples don't start with the knowledge, skill, strength, and maturity of character successful relationships require. For the most part, it's on-the-job training. Personal history, level of education, or any of the other factors many people assume are determining aspects of committed partnerships don't accurately predict the likelihood of relationship success. It's in the cauldron of commitment that we can promote the strengthening of the essential qualities these relationships thrive on.

This is a partial list, but it includes qualities we believe are most important:

- Generosity
- Humility
- Responsibility
- Integrity
- Humor
- Vulnerability

- Honesty
- Compassion
- Courage
- Self-trust
- Adventurousness
- Patience

You get to choose whether or not you want to go for the gold that can be found in committed partnerships. And if you make that choice, one of the skills essential to this process is the ability to navigate the territory of relationship differences effectively. We've written this book to help you do just that. The next step is up to you.

1.

Yes, it really is possible to avoid arguments.

When it comes to relationships, differences are inevitable, but conflict is optional. The real question is exactly how we avoid conflict when differences in our beliefs, preferences, and sometimes even values show up in our close relationships. Differences are not only a certainty but a necessity for the "chemistry" that fuels attraction. We don't attract people who are more like us, because people who are just like us would not have as much to offer in terms of learning, healing, and other aspects of personal development. People who are just like us aren't as interesting as those with whom we don't share identical traits. While familiarity and predictability are desirable, too much of a good thing can breed boredom, stagnation, or even resentment. To maximize the development potential of a relationship, it must also include differences to challenge as well as comfort, to provoke as well as support, and to enliven as well as reassure.

Differences provide the catalyst for these experiences but can turn into arguments when both parties attempt to coerce each other into their perspectives. A simple difference of opinion can degrade a relationship if it isn't resolved. Hurts don't disappear when there is no resolution; they just go underground, where they quietly breed mistrust. Using manipulative tactics to coerce another into agreement amplifies the problem. Examples of manipulation include intimidation, threats (explicit or implicit), making demands, yelling, going silent, blaming, interrupting, guilt-tripping, intellectualizing, or shaming, to name a few.

Fear underlies nearly all coercive strategies. Generally, the fear represents concern that the outcome of the interaction will result in a loss of love, power, respect, or control if our partner's will prevails. It could also have to do with an anticipated loss of protection that would leave us vulnerable to punishment, rejection, or injury.

When faced with this threat, a variety of fears can be activated that may awaken memories of past losses or trauma. We all learn to develop strategies for protection as a result of these early experiences in the hopes of preventing future suffering. Arguments represent an effort by both parties to protect themselves from the possibility of domination and exploitation. The thinking usually goes something like "As long as I am disagreeing with you, I am minimizing or eliminating the possibility of being harmed, and am also more likely to win you over to my side."

As the saying goes, "It takes two to tango." Have you ever seen one person dance the tango? Probably not, and you're not likely to. Neither are you likely to observe an argument in which only one person is arguing. "Just don't argue back" is the simple answer to how to avoid an argument. The problem with that answer is that it's almost impossible to not argue when someone close tries to convert us to a point of view that we don't agree with.

Simply clamming up generally doesn't seem like a sufficiently strong response to affirm our perspective. This raises the question "Why then is it so important to go on the record and announce that we don't see things the same way?"

If we don't make it clear that we disagree with the other person, we are likely to fear that they will assume our silence implies agreement, and this belief can lead to serious complications. The problem with arguing with another's point of view is that the possibility for mutual understanding disappears. Until and unless the intention of the conversation moves from defensiveness to openness, an argument will inevitably ensue.

Many people are so accustomed to proceeding down that slippery slope that it's difficult to conceive of having differing points of view without having arguments. Holding this perspective creates a self-fulfilling prophecy that makes arguments inevitable. At such times, the motivation to develop the skills necessary for creating a conscious dialogue is minimal at best. However, our experience confirms the possibility that such outcomes can and do occur.

Being open involves the willingness to be vulnerable. This requires us to disarm ourselves of the emotional protection we believe our defensiveness provides. Disengaging from defensiveness always feels risky. Paradoxically, that very vulnerability provides the key to breaking the impasse created by our mutual defensiveness.

Vulnerability rarely feels comfortable and is an acquired taste that can be cultivated. If one is willing to be vulnerable, conflict can be avoided in most cases. If you're thinking that this is easier said than done, you're right! But "not easy" is a far cry from "not possible." If you're ready to accept the challenge, congratulations!

2.

Practice does not necessarily make perfect, but it sure helps.

Becoming skilled in any endeavor requires the building of skills necessary for competence and mastery.

The general principles include (but are not limited to) . . .

- Practice
- Commitment
- Learning
- Training
- Practice
- Technical guidance
- Practice
- Prioritizing
- Oh, did we mention practice?

In case you're not familiar with the definition of the word *practice*, here is Webster's version: "repeated exercise in or performance of an activity or skill so as to acquire or maintain proficiency in it." The key word here is *repeated*. To develop competency in any area of life, we need to practice. Books and workshops can definitely help, but there's no better way to pit ourselves against the challenges relationships provide than actually being in one.

Despite the old saying that "practice makes perfect," in most cases it doesn't. Even the most gifted musicians, doctors, writers, actors, and others who stand out in their chosen field rarely if ever see themselves as flawless in their performance, even though others may see them that way.

The development of any new skill involves the process of moving forward and then slipping backward, repeatedly. That's where patience comes in. If we expect a steady path upwards to mastery, we're likely to be disappointed and eventually may stop practicing. Although most people would prefer to avoid conflict altogether, the likelihood of doing so is extremely low. Consequently, learning to manage differences before they turn into destructive combat is probably a good idea.

We won't always be able to stay present, conscious, and centered, but we can learn how to recover when we get thrown off track. It's possible to recover so quickly that no one but ourselves even notices that we temporarily lost it. But this takes practice, and that means that we have to be willing to experience being thrown—not literally thrown like a practicing martial artist, but thrown off our internal center, which happens when we lose our sense of emotional balance. Every instance of "losing it" in an argument represents another opportunity to practice getting it back.

This happens more quickly, and with less effort, once we override the old habit of reacting with defensiveness and/or offensiveness. Our new default becomes an impulse to . . .

- Experience the feeling that is being activated
- Breathe
- Identify the feeling
- Take a moment to pause and reflect
- Communicate your experience to your partner
- Repeat until you either feel more complete or need to take a break

Misunderstandings come up at least occasionally for everyone, but they need not derail us. And even if they do, we can put ourselves back on track by focusing on what we can do to get re-railed rather than what the other person did that threw us off. The realization that we can be effective agents in this process rather than helpless victims is a game-changer. Once we see this, not just as an intellectual construct but from the results of our experience, it's hard to ever go back. But then, why would you want to?

3.

From breakdown to breakthrough

A relationship breakdown is an unexpected interruption that leaves one or both partners feeling, angry, disappointed, hurt, or in some way incomplete. It often involves a broken agreement, lie, betrayal, or a misunderstanding.

How likely are we to experience breakdowns in relationship? Since we are human beings, approximately 100 percent. Consequently, a reasonable strategy would be to learn to manage breakdowns when they inevitably occur. Many people want to believe that they can be the exception to this rule, and that it is possible to avoid having breakdowns by denying differences. But this strategy will only defer the breakdown to a later date.

Another strategy is faultfinding, which creates a cycle of blame and defensiveness. While we use our grievances as "evidence" that our partner has punitive intentions, they may be doing the same thing. They could be reacting from fear and trying to protect themselves from a perceived threat.

What determines whether we can transform a breakdown to a breakthrough is our ability to replace an intention to protect with an intention to learn. Doing so will reveal areas of mistrust that need to be addressed in order to restore good faith. Consider the breakdown of Chad and Leslie.

Chad and Leslie got tickets to go to a videotaping of a national celebrity at their local public TV station. On the day of the taping,

Leslie had professional appointments all morning and knew they were cutting it close to arrive at the studio by the designated time of 2 PM. She ran over time in planning their departure and didn't get Chad's message about needing extra time for parking. They got stuck in heavy traffic and were both tense the whole drive, fearing they would be late. They had trouble finding the TV studio, and then had difficulty locating a parking space. Leslie asked to be dropped off at the station, but Chad refused her request, claiming that it was in a bad part of town. After finally finding a parking space, they ran all the way to the studio but arrived at three minutes after two, just after the door closed.

Leslie: "We both felt terrible. I was furious with Chad for being overprotective when he wouldn't let me out of the car, but I resisted my impulse to lash out at him. I also felt guilty about leaving the house late. I had made Chad miss something that was important to him. I was afraid that he would blame me."

Chad: "This kind of breakdown would have, in the past, created a terrible argument that might have gone on for days. We had both been practicing replacing blame with responsibility, and I had been practicing self-restraint to manage my angry outbursts. So, we spent the next couple of hours working with everything that this disappointment flushed up."

Leslie: "We both knew that if there was this much deep feeling around one incident, there must be a lot more going on."

Chad: "We spent two hours on my refusal to let Leslie walk through the inner city. I discovered that my attitude had changed since the birth of our child last year. Now I felt more protective."

Leslie: "I got in touch with some of my mixed feelings about becoming a mother. On the one hand I enjoyed being doted on, but on the other hand, I resented being treated like a weakling."

Chad: "Both of us got in touch with a lot of feelings we didn't even know were there until the breakdown occurred and ripped the lid off. It was hard to open up to all those emotions, but the experience left us both feeling much closer to each other."

This incident provides an example of how situations that may initially appear disastrous can prove to be a blessing when they are approached with a desire to connect rather than protect, and to learn rather than control. This breakdown was relatively minor. Some breakdowns are more serious and may take much longer to repair. But no matter how small a breakdown may be, the opportunity is always available to practice on the little pains so that when bigger ordeals occur, we have become more skilled in our ability to handle them. Handling breakdowns has been compared to doing detective work. It is a search for clues that might reveal what is going on below the surface of our relationship, undertaken with an intention to discover what is fueling our reactivity and attend to it rather than focus on our partner's "misbehavior."

The bigger the crisis, the bigger the challenge. But also the bigger the opportunity for growth. Big breakdowns can really shake up a relationship, and life as we have known it can feel shattered. But if we can bring an attitude that values learning over combativeness, our relationship can not only survive the inevitable bumps in the road but also grow to become more mutually fulfilling. Just ask Leslie and Chad.

4.

Transforming desire into intention

Intention comes from the Latin *intendere*, which means "to stretch towards." This is the source of the energy that moves us towards our desired outcome. There is an important distinction between "desire" and "intention." Desire has to do with a longing for something, someone, or for a particular experience. An intention has to do with a purpose, upon which one's mind is concentrated. While desire is primarily a state of feeling, intention adds not only strength to that feeling but a commitment to take whatever action is necessary for the fulfillment of that desire.

This distinction is not surprising for anyone who has ever experienced an intention to fulfill a desire. Intentions generally require us to stretch our limits, sometimes to what can feel like the breaking point. The vast majority of our desires remain just that, desires, simply because adding the element of commitment requires us to be willing to stretch ourselves beyond the edges of our comfort zone and take risks that we ordinarily would try to avoid. Intentions have to do with extraordinary experiences in which the desire level is so strong that we feel compelled to exert ourselves in order to fulfill our purpose.

It's notable that the dictionary uses the word *stretch* rather than *move* in reference to the necessity to extend ourselves and to be willing "to exert our efforts to the utmost." Commitment adds the critical ingredient that mobilizes the energy to bring forth the desired outcome. And commitment is a way of being that embodies determination to fulfill a specific purpose.

Regardless of why we choose what to be committed to or even whether commitment is a choice that we consciously make, when we are operating from an intention, our desired outcome is much more likely to be fulfilled than when we are not. That is at least in part because we have put more of ourselves into the process of fulfilling our commitment.

So, what determines how committed we are? It has to do with how important something is to us—the degree to which we believe the attainment of our goal will enhance the quality of our life. If we doubt that the fulfillment of our goal is realistic or even possible for us, then making a heroic effort makes no sense, and consequently we are unlikely to stretch towards that goal. In fact, our desired outcome may never even make it into the category of a goal and will remain an unrealizable fantasy.

What may the biggest obstacle for those who have been unsuccessful in creating truly meaningful relationships is the belief that it is unrealistic to possess high expectations. They believe that not having lofty expectations prevents them from experiencing failure or the disappointment that accompanies a lack of success in the fulfillment of a desire. While denying what we really want may seem to protect us from these feelings and provide a great rationale for staying in our comfort zone, a hefty price tag comes with the "comfort" they provide. Lowered expectations create a self-fulfilling prophecy that inevitably leads to an affirmation of the belief that we're destined to live out our life without a truly loving partnership.

Turning a desire into an intention requires the willingness to risk the disappointment we are trying to avoid. We can challenge our protective impulses by countering the "evidence" we've used as proof that there's no point in even trying. Most of what we see as proof is speculation based upon our past history, which is not necessarily a reliable prediction of the future. Freeing ourselves from the grip of resignation that this belief promotes is a surefire way to create a relationship future that is different from our past.

We have all, at times, been convinced that we were right about something that turned out not to be true, something we couldn't do or achieve, and somehow we did. Releasing ourselves from this conviction is the first—but certainly not the last—step in the process of turning a desire into an intention and an intention into a reality. It's actually a form of arrogance to get so attached to our belief that we disqualify any evidence to the contrary without considering its validity. Admitting that we may not always be right about what we believe requires humility, as well as the courage to risk exposing ourselves to the possibility of feeling the disappointment that can come from failure.

The best way to avoid failure is to avoid trying in the first place. But doing that makes another, even bigger kind of failure inevitable: that is, the failure to even try. We can minimize conflict in our relationships by convincing ourselves that we're just not good at dealing with differences. Or we can take the risk and arm ourselves with some tools our intention has helped us to acquire and get back in the game. It's up to each of us to choose.

5.

To vent or not to vent

Charlie: In the early years of our relationship, Linda and I believed in the theory that it is best to express anger immediately, directly, and strongly to the person with whom you're upset. This provided me with a convenient justification for converting all of my more vulnerable emotions (like fear, disappointment, sadness, shame, desire, etc.) into anger and dumping them on Linda. It felt familiar and safe for me to do so. And since I was more experienced with blaming, shaming, and raising my voice at people than she was, this worked pretty well for me. At least, it seemed to, until Linda let me know that it wasn't working so well for her.

Unfortunately, by that time a lot of damage had been done to our relationship. After all, I came from a family in which blasting others with anger was considered a reasonable response to getting upset. Consequently, I felt not only comfortable venting my anger towards Linda but completely justified in doing so. It's not easy to admit that I was nothing more than a bully picking on someone who was no match for me when it came to intimidation.

Linda: Unlike Charlie, I grew up in a family where children were punished for expressing anger towards anyone, particularly adults. Talking back to a parent could easily result in harsh punishment. I learned that if I were to survive, I would have to become a master at concealing any feelings that had the potential to cause distress to my parents.

Charlie: In graduate school in the seventies, Linda and I were exposed to a school of thought that came out of the encounter movement, in which projecting negative emotions onto others was seen as therapeutic. This further legitimatized what had by now become a dysfunctional pattern of hostility and defensiveness in our marriage. Then I got a job facilitating personal-growth workshops in which catharsis, a process in which repressed emotions are expressed outwardly, was an important part of the seminars.

Linda: By this time, having survived and learned from a great many encounters with Charlie, I had overcome enough of my fear of confrontation to be willing to stand up to him rather than cave in. While this was definitely a step in the right direction, there was still more work for both of us to do. We knew that to co-create the kind of relationship we wanted, we would have to replace our method of dealing with our differences with a more workable system. We were fortunate enough to find some gifted teachers who believed that healing does not come from venting anger but rather is a function of incorporating greater openheartedness, honesty, and vulnerability into the relationship.

Since then, we've not only put the painful past behind us, we've experienced a degree of trust and goodwill in our marriage that goes beyond anything either of us had ever experienced or even imagined. We learned that attacking others is never productive and discovered some hard research data from studies about conflict that affirmed what we'd concluded from our personal experience. In his groundbreaking book *Human Aggression*, researcher Russell Geen found that while "blowing off steam" at another person may provide temporary relief, it is also likely to amplify underlying feelings of hostility, which may provoke retaliation and escalation. According to Geen, what happens during repeated expressions of intense anger towards another is that inhibitions against violence are lowered, resulting in people becoming more hostile. In addition, feelings of guilt and anxiety tend to arise after one has unloaded their wrath onto another. Letting off steam generally makes people more, not less, angry and leaves them with a lot of repair work to do in order to restore lost or damaged trust, goodwill, and respect.

Many people see only two options: blow it out or stuff it. Fortunately, there is a third option. It is possible to express intense feelings in ways that neither attack nor threaten. We can turn down the heat while expressing our feelings without blame or name-calling. We can seek to create an outcome in which both parties are satisfied with the result rather than one in which there is a winner and a loser. Expressing anger without accusation or an intention to retaliate opens the door to having a respectful dialogue instead of one characterized by fear or defensiveness. One way to do this is to make statements that are grounded in our own experience instead of our judgment of our partner's behavior. Here are examples of this: "I'm really disappointed that you forgot my birthday," "I'm frustrated and angry that we're going around in circles again," and "It scares me when you say you think that maybe we're just not meant to be together."

This solution requires assertiveness rather than aggression, vulnerability rather than defensiveness, and responsibility rather than blame. Admittedly, this is no easy thing to do, particularly in the heat of an intense emotional exchange; but with practice, these traits can be developed.

Perhaps the most compelling factor in any tendency to indulge in anger is the assumption that leading with aggression makes one less vulnerable. Conventional wisdom suggests that the best defense is a good offense and advises us to "fight fire with fire." While this philosophy may work well when it comes to contact sports, in terms of personal relationships, it's a surefire recipe for disaster. Aggression is much more likely to activate hostility and counterattacks than is vulnerability, which often defuses defensiveness.

Vulnerability cools things down, which is what we need to do when things get overheated. Although we may believe that counterattacking will make us feel safer, generally the opposite is true. If we want more openness, trust, and intimacy in our relationship, being vulnerable is what it takes. If not, we can always keep fighting. It's our choice.

6.

Nonreactive listening

J uan and Mercedes came into marriage counseling clueless as to why there was so much pain and suffering in their relationship. After listening to each of them describe their situation, it soon became obvious what the problem was. Neither could say anything about the other without lacing statements with harsh judgments and criticism. They were both brought up in families in which this type of communication was common, and neither of them knew that it was possible to respond to hurtful words with anything other than defensiveness or a counterattack. They also didn't realize how damaging this form of communication was to their feelings of trust and mutual respect. Nearly every conversation quickly deteriorated into a frenzy of name-calling that left them both feeling wounded and resentful.

Destructive cycles like this inevitably result in prolonged suffering and often in divorce if the pattern is not interrupted. The constant wear and tear on the fabric of the partnership erodes the goodwill that was once present and threatens not only the integrity of the relationship but the health and well-being of both partners. The stress they each experience is both emotionally and physically damaging. It's not an exaggeration to compare the participants in this type of ongoing interaction to victims of PTSD (post-traumatic stress disorder). They each, however, are perpetrators as well as victims in this cycle, and they will continue to be until they take responsibility for interrupting their own reactive tendencies rather than focusing on what their partner is doing to cause them to become defensive.

When we feel attacked or unjustly blamed for something, the impulse to react can feel overwhelmingly compelling, even impossible to resist. We want to defend ourselves, often by counterattacking or making an accusation to deflect the pain of the attack we have received or anticipate receiving. It takes courage to respond nondefensively when we feel wounded, more courage than it takes to fight back. But keep in mind, not fighting back doesn't mean we are giving in or admitting we're wrong. It simply means that we are not trying to persuade our partner that we're right or punish them for having caused us to feel hurt, angry, or threatened.

While it does ultimately take two to restore a broken relationship to a state of wholeness, it only takes one to end the destructive attack/defend/counterattack cycle. When one person embodies authentic honesty and vulnerability in the face of hostility, in most cases, aggressive impulses cool down. It doesn't necessarily happen immediately, which is why it feels like a risk to drop a protective strategy in the face of a perceived threat.

And yet it is possible for anyone with a clear intention to take steps in this direction. Nonreactive listening requires a high degree of self-restraint, but with practice (for which relationships generally provide lots of opportunities), this skill can develop relatively quickly. Even after an angry comment has been blurted out, nonreactive listening can keep the situation from descending into the hell zone.

For example, imagine that your partner sharply criticized your parenting. Rather than defensively insisting that you are *not* a bad parent, you could acknowledge that your partner has concerns about your parenting style and that you are open to hearing them, but only if they can be stated in ways that are not personally condemning.

Another option is to speak from your own experience and let your partner know how their attack impacted you. You could say, for instance, "I know that you're upset with me and I'm open to listening to your concerns, but when you hurl insults at me, it's very hard for me to stay open. Can you tell me more about what it is that you're needing?"

There is nothing wrong with expressing opinions. People do it all the time, and often that can lead to worthwhile discussions. But when the opinion is about the other person rather than the content of what they said, it's more likely that one or both people will feel misunderstood and upset. When these feelings are present, the urge to react defensively is likely to be strong. Counterattacking makes us feel less vulnerable and more protected, and it's not easy to override this hardwired tendency. We may wonder, "Why should I turn the other cheek when I feel attacked?" or "Why shouldn't I react by putting my partner in their place?" or "What kind of person would allow themselves to be attacked without attempting to defend themselves?"

These are important questions that each of us needs to consider. In choosing an appropriate response to feeling attacked, it comes down to what our intention is in the moment. If our intention is to create a safer, more respectful, and trusting environment within the relationship, then resisting the temptation to counterattack is the smartest thing we can do. Judgments, unsolicited opinions, advice, criticism, blame, faultfinding, name-calling, and other types of verbal violence are all forms of aggression. When we meet aggression with aggression, feelings of fear and anger become amplified. When this happens, we both feel more threatened, and less safe, thus perpetuating the cycle.

Even for those who understand that fighting verbal violence with verbal violence only creates more suffering, vulnerability in the face of a perceived attack can feel very risky. The problem for many, even those who sincerely want to break this cycle, is that we don't feel that we can. When we feel threatened, it's easy to think that the only alternative to being reactive is to be passive. Passivity is a state of inertia in the face of danger. It's a strategy for dealing with an underlying feeling of helplessness. As an alternative to the aggression/passivity dichotomy, we can take an active but nonaggressive stance to assert our truth during an emotional confrontation. To do so, we need to know what this truth is.

This isn't easy in the face of strong emotions. When someone shows up as a threat, it's easy to perceive them as the enemy. If we take our eyes off an adversary, he or she may exploit that momentary lapse of attention. If we are dealing with a real enemy who poses a genuine threat, it may be appropriate to maintain this external focus until we feel safe. If we make the assessment that someone's primary intention is to cause harm or exploit us in order to serve their own agenda, openness in such a situation would be inappropriate, even foolish.

In redirecting our attention away from another and towards ourselves, we become more aware of our current experience, which enables us to be more present, grounded, and responsive to the challenges of the moment, rather than reacting from our defensive programming.

If we become too activated to do this, we can call for a time-out to cool down, after which we can resume the dialogue. We might say something like "I need a few minutes to think about that," "I'm taking a brief break, but I'll be back," "I'm so upset right now I can't hear what you're saying," or "I need a break to calm myself down." In all these examples, because the speaker is taking responsibility for his or her experience and not blaming the other person, it is likely that these statements will be met with acceptance rather than continued attack. Connecting to our own experience is the best thing we can do in the midst of a strong emotional exchange. It inevitably de-escalates hostility. Defensive patterns don't dissolve instantly, but with practice and over time, they can be put in their place. The payoffs are worth the effort.

7.

Adults sometimes need time-outs too.

When our kids were small, we had a tool for averting a blowup over their behavior: a time-out. A tried-and-true instrument in most parents' tool bag, a time-out is an interruption of a situation that is going downhill fast. It's a cooling-off period that can provide relief from an increasingly agitated interaction. This time allows both parties to gain their composure and eventually reengage when calmer heads prevail.

Over the years of working with couples, it has become evident to us that children are not the only ones who occasionally need time-outs. In fact, most couples have multiple incidents over the course of their relationship in which taking a time-out can prove beneficial.

Certain topics of conversation between couples can trigger strong emotional reactions; money, sex, child-rearing, parents and in-laws, eating habits, weight control, and driving habits are all hot-button subjects that can deteriorate into destructive arguments. Even under the best of conditions, with the best of intentions, a partner can unknowingly activate a land mine, with explosive results. If one tries but fails to repair the damage, a time-out may be called for in order to cool down before resuming the conversation.

Intentionality is an essential part of any effective time-out. During this time, each partner sets the intention to settle themselves down, to defuse their emotions so they can reunite, ready to hear the other person without reacting with judgment, blame, or defensiveness. This level of vulnerability is almost impossible to achieve when in the grip of intense emotions. When both partners have adjusted their attitude, they increase their chances of having a mutually satisfying interaction.

There is no "correct" amount of time for a time-out break. Some situations require no more than a couple of minutes to take a few breaths. Sometimes it can take an hour or more, depending on the circumstances and the nature of the breakdown. It's not uncommon for one person to require more time than the other to calm overheated emotions. It's best not to go much longer than an hour so that the discussion is fresh in each partner's mind. In cases that require more time, don't go over twenty-four hours, no matter what the issue is. Keep in mind, the object of a time-out is not necessarily to resolve the issue once and for all. It's simply to prevent the situation from further deteriorating, and to continue the dialogue with greater openness, respect, and committed listening.

To reiterate, the presence of differences in relationships is inevitable. Conflict is optional. Differences become conflict when one or both partners try to coerce the other into agreeing with their view or accommodating their expectations. Even couples with great relationships occasionally experience breakdowns. The difference is that in the early stages of a disagreement, they are able to interrupt the downward spiral, thus preventing disaster. The way we initiate a time-out and take our leave is of utmost importance. If we stalk off, stamping our feet, scowling, or slamming the door, we're unlikely to bring about a successful reconciliation. It's also helpful to have an understanding that either partner has the authority at any time to initiate a break when they feel the need for it, no questions asked.

While the solution to conflict is often to have more communication, sometimes the opposite is true, and what's needed is a pause in communication, particularly during those times when your best efforts seem to be making things worse. Trying harder doesn't always help.

Sometimes letting go of our efforts and regrouping is the best path to greater mutual understanding and receptivity. The ability to know when to let go and when to press on can be cultivated over time and through experience. Like anything worthwhile, it doesn't occur overnight, but given sufficient motivation and commitment, it will enhance the quality of any relationship. Guaranteed!

8.

The victim

When we feel pain, we want to identify its source so we can end it and prevent future suffering. We instinctively withdraw our hand from the hot frying pan handle or take a couple of aspirin to ease the pain of a headache. In the case of a relationship, we blame the person that we think has caused pain in the hope that doing so will make us less likely to be hurt again. But while blaming our partner may make us feel protected from future pain, that protection is usually an illusion rather than a guarantee. In identifying someone as a "perpetrator," we automatically identify ourselves as a victim, which comes with its own set of difficulties.

Whether in a relationship or outside of it, we are not suggesting that dangerous people don't exist in the world and that we don't need to be mindful of whom we trust. The question is, can we discern whom to trust without taking on the victim identity?

Most of us have had the experience of feeling like a victim. But there are consequences to adopting that persona and relating to the world—or our partner—from that position. Yet many are quick to adopt that identity when it comes to circumstances in which we feel we've been taken advantage of or harmed. We may have fallen prey to someone looking to fulfill his or her own (usually concealed) desires for personal gain at our expense. If this is the case, we will understandably feel victimized. Feeling victimized and embodying the identity of a victim are, however, two different things.

If we feel like a victim or identify ourselves as one, whether we realize it or not, we carry that attitude around with us. Ironically, doing so makes us more, not less, vulnerable to the attention of potential predators, who are generally adept at picking up nonverbal cues of vulnerability in others. The more predatory a person is, the more easily they can identify potential victims. When we internalize an identity as opposed to temporarily experiencing a feeling, that identity inevitably manifests itself in our behavior; there's an unconscious tendency to act in ways that are consistent with it.

If we see ourselves as a victim, we are inclined to interpret the acts of others as deliberately harmful, whether they are or not. There could be some truth to our concerns, but these expectations feel more like reality than suspicions. Having a victim identity can result in a self-fulfilling prophecy in which we collect examples that validate our worldview of victims and perpetrators.

Many adopt a victim identity despite the obvious downside of doing so. The reasons include . . .

- A feeling of security that comes with a victim's sense that they're aware of dangers lurking.
- A victim is not responsible for their actions and thus can't be blamed.
- Victims feel justified in retaliating towards those who they feel have abused them.
- Victims often feel morally superior to perpetrators.
- Victims often believe that they're incapable of intentionally harming others.

These so-called "benefits" don't come without a price. These prices include . . .

- A feeling of powerlessness that comes with the denial of responsibility
- Prolonged self-pity that inhibits emotional availability

- A tendency to doubt one's ability to provide self-care
- A diminished capacity to accurately assess the trustworthiness of others
- A feeling of increased loneliness that is fostered by a belief that the world is dangerous

For those who would like to recover from a victim identity, here are a few guidelines that can help free you from its grip:

- Cultivate friendships with people who do not reinforce your feelings of being a victim.
- Ask your friends to not just provide you with sympathy but also help you to see ways in which you may have had something to do with your situation.
- Request that they help you see the lessons you have not recognized and figure out how to apply them in the future. Friends and family often mean well but may be blinded by their loyalty to us.
- Don't believe everything you think. Thoughts may seem like they are "the truth" when in fact they may be no more than imaginings.
- Behave in ways that help you develop a sense of self-trust, and remind yourself of the benefits you will enjoy from breaking free of a false identity.

It can't be overemphasized that people do get victimized. All of us have had experiences in which we were, through no fault of our own, treated unfairly and physically or emotionally wounded. When we no longer identify ourselves as a victim, others relate to us with greater openness. Interpersonal conflict diminishes greatly because we no longer see others as adversaries but rather see them as individuals who themselves are trying to get their own needs met. And this shift in our perspective can be a real game-changer!

9.

Are you conflict avoidant?

"A failure to confront is a failure to love."

—M. Scott Peck, MD

Who has never found themselves in conflict with another person? It could be a friend, relative, life partner, coworker, or anyone with whom we are experiencing a difference of opinion. Given the fact that humans hold different perspectives regarding beliefs, values, and even perception of reality, it's a wonder that we don't have more conflicts than we do. While some seem to welcome and even deliberately create antagonism in relationships, others may do everything in their power to avoid conflict. We may fear confrontation because we think our partner will get angry or hurt if we attempt to discuss a problem or stand up for ourselves. But over time, this avoidance may leave us feeling hurt, anxious, or resentful.

If you think you might be a conflict avoider, you've come to the right page. This chapter will also be helpful to those in a relationship with a conflict avoider because you'll learn how to make it safer for them to engage in conversations that are potentially anxiety provoking. If you're not sure if you are a conflict avoider, reading this chapter will help you find out. Here are some questions to think about:

- Do you generally consider angry feelings dangerous?
- Do you withdraw in silence when speaking up is called for?
- Do you avoid declaring what you think and feel to keep those around you comfortable?

- Do you, at times, sacrifice your sense of reality in an attempt to preserve harmony?
- Are you spending so much time scanning for what others are feeling and thinking that you fail to recognize your own experience?
- Do you find yourself complaining, but nothing really changes?
- Have you created a mountain of unfinished business by avoiding necessary conversations?
- Do you make others' needs and desires more important than your own?
- Do you find yourself taking responsibility for others' reactions?
- When things go wrong, is your initial impulse to think that it must be your fault?
- Is the approval of others more important to you than your feelings of self-worth?

If you answered yes to at least half of these questions, there's a good chance that you have a tendency to avoid conflict. You have already taken the first step by honestly looking at yourself. One reason why it's hard to overcome conflict aversion is that there are obvious advantages to it. And yet there's a price to be paid for automatically defaulting to it. Some of the disadvantages are as follows:

- Becoming so used to avoidance that you do it even in situations that *are* worth taking a stand for
- Reinforcing the belief that you are incapable of dealing with differences in a productive way
- A diminishment in your level of self-respect
- A diminishment of the level of respect others hold towards you
- An increase in your level of insecurity and anxiety

The good news is that in recognizing that you may be a conflict avoider, you have interrupted the pattern of denial. You've told yourself the truth: that you have some responsibility for this problem and that there is something you can do about it.

For example:

- Practice self-forgiveness for the times you have judged or punished yourself in some way because you felt weak. Being a conflict avoider is nothing to be ashamed of. Most people have issues with conflict, even those who attempt to intimidate others with threats and aggression. They have just chosen to deal with their fear differently than you have.
- Forgive those towards whom you have harbored resentment or punished by direct or passive means.
- Tell the truth. Compile a list of people in your life, starting with your most important relationships, with whom you have withheld your feelings. Recognize that in being untruthful, you have accumulated resentment that has contributed to a diminishment of mutual trust and respect. Make a list of specific resentments you hold towards each person.
- Give yourself permission to feel the resentment, anger, outrage, or whatever other feelings you have not permitted yourself to fully experience, and identify the fear that kept you from feeling it.
- Take responsibility for your part in the creation of your conflict-phobia.
- Invite the other person to join you in a conversation about "some things that I've been needing to talk to you about for a while." Note: you need not use these words, but try to issue the invitation as a request rather than a demand. The tone of your words is more important than the words themselves.
- Apologize. If you feel remorse about something you've done or said, tell the truth.
- Respectfully declare your intention. Let the other person know why it is important to you to communicate your concerns and what you hope to accomplish by doing so.
- And finally, thank your partner for joining you in your efforts to enhance the quality of your relationship.

Addressing certain issues with someone can sometimes evoke a defensive response. If it does, they may be afraid that they're being accused of doing something wrong and that they'll be punished if found guilty. Their fear can be defused if we can remain nonreactive.

Admittedly, this process takes practice. But with gentle persistence, defensive patterns can be dissolved, allowing for authentic and truly meaningful connections. Like any other pattern, recovery from the habit of conflict avoidance requires intentionality and commitment. It starts with the decision to finally become free of our fears. When we see that we can honor our own truth without getting into a destructive interchange, we can engage directly, honestly, and ultimately, fearlessly. Are you ready?

10.

Why winning doesn't work

Although arguments can't always be prevented, it is possible to argue in ways that produce productive rather than destructive outcomes and result in enhanced mutual understanding, trust, and respect. Bringing about such an outcome requires that we begin with an intention to do so. Making a conscious choice enables us to override any attitudes that may predispose us to bring a negative perspective characterized by pessimism or resignation to our interaction.

If we have a history of failures in our efforts to bring about successful resolutions to differences, we are likely to default to a sense of hopelessness, increasing the likelihood of this argument turning out like most of our previous ones have. An attitude of cynicism can protect us from experiencing another disappointing outcome. Unfortunately, this attitude can lead to a self-fulfilling prophecy.

Many couples get into power struggles out of their desires to control each other. There are no winners here. When one "wins" or gets their way through disrespectful means such as intimidation, coercion, dishonesty, or other forms of manipulation, there is an inevitable diminishment of goodwill, respect, and integrity in the relationship. These diminishments will show up in many ways, both overt and covert. One way or another, they will negatively impact the couple's quality of connection.

When one or both partners are guided by an intention to create mutual satisfaction rather than an intention to "win the battle," there is a much greater likelihood of a favorable outcome. And although in the long run it does take two to co-create this transformation, it only takes one to risk vulnerability and take the first step to initiate the process.

The more we see life as a process of making choices rather than fulfilling external expectations, the less inclined we are to feel victimized and disempowered, both of which are feelings that prompt a need for greater control to compensate for perceived helplessness. Indulging in excuse making and blaming reinforces feelings that predispose us towards controlling behaviors. The alternative to this self-defeating program is the willingness to accept responsibility for the choices that we make and to live with (and hopefully learn from) the consequences of our decisions. In doing this, our partner no longer feels that he or she is being viewed as "the problem" and is likely to be open to engaging in a mutually respectful dialogue.

It's not *because* of our protective strategies that we still have a relationship but *despite* them. As with other habits, we often develop repetitive patterns of thought and behavior associated with survival. Because few of us develop alternative ways of effectively dealing with these patterns, issues around conflict tend to be the number one cause of relationship breakdowns. Anything done in order to gain dominance rather than mutual satisfaction diminishes the quality of connection for both partners. If one wins at the other's expense, both lose. On the other hand, if we sacrifice our own well-being to accommodate our partner, the net result is the same.

In order for there to be a successful resolution to any situation that involves conflicting desires, two things have to be present: (1) a commitment to both people experiencing some degree of satisfaction; and (2) a means through which that outcome can be realized. We refer to these patterns as "survival strategies" because we might feel that our very survival is at stake, particularly when our partner's desire threatens to prevent us from experiencing something deemed vital to our well-being. When we disable this emergency alarm system, we interrupt the impulse to control. This can break the pattern of fight/flight/freeze, which turns a win-lose game into a cooperative team effort.

Doing so requires a clear intention on both partners' parts to give up the notion that winning is the object of the game. Yet even those who have been stuck for years or decades in the win-lose paradigm can reach a point at which it becomes painfully evident that this system just isn't working. Ironically, the point at which we feel the most hopeless might be the moment we find the motivation to take the leap of faith that this transformation requires. It just depends on how tired we are of going down that particular rabbit hole.

11.

Negotiation

You may have heard, as we have, a lot of dissatisfaction—and even cynicism—about marriage these days. In recent years, social sanctions against divorce have diminished. The glue of the old rules is no longer holding. This is not necessarily a bad thing, since it has resulted in a general acceptance that some marriages are best dissolved. Still, many people believe that the pendulum swinging between unconditional, permanent commitment and no-fault divorce may have swung too far.

A prevailing attitude towards marriage can be described as "whatever works." Each couple is left to design a form of marriage that works for them. But while the old form of marriage has been forsaken, new forms have not yet been established. In these precarious times, we are called upon to design the next ways of being in partnership that will bring the deep satisfaction everyone seeks.

Rigid role responsibilities have relaxed; consequently, more discussion and greater negotiation skills are needed to work out questions and concerns that were not even present in the traditional model of marriage. Having lofty goals is a good thing. But holding and fulfilling great expectations requires vision, commitment, and a strong sense of personal responsibility.

Many of us have a good work ethic when it comes to career. Yet some have the mistaken notion that their work ethic doesn't apply when it comes to personal partnerships. They may believe the romantic myth that love is enough to ensure happiness throughout their marriage. Such magical thinking inevitably leads to great disappointment. It fails to take into account the communication, conflict management, and negotiation skills required for optimal partnerships. When these misguided beliefs remain unexamined, they can run our relationship into the ground.

Today, the challenge is to envision a new form of marriage, one in which both people can develop into the best that they can be, and each has greater authority to define the nature of their unique concerns and mutual agreements. It's not only likely but also inevitable that there will be some discomfort in approaching a new way of conceptualizing relationships. Marriage is a commitment designed to hold our feet to the fire. Without this commitment, the option to walk away would be difficult to resist, especially during trying times. And while some marriages can't be saved, many can, given a willingness of both partners to dedicate themselves to finding creative solutions to their challenges.

A few of the practices couples can engage in to develop effective negotiation skills are as follows:

- Using "I" statements when referring to perceptions, feelings, thoughts, and needs
- Listening nonreactively and nondefensively
- Clarifying specific expectations and the degree of importance of your concerns
- Creating and keeping agreed-upon guidelines for successful conversations
- Acknowledging each interaction that moves the process forward
- Interrupting your impulse to interrupt the other person
- Focus more on your intended outcome rather than trying to invalidate your partner's views
- Hold a spirit of fairness and reciprocity as a theme of your negotiations

These skills not only enhance the well-being of romantic

partnerships, but they are also transferable to other relationships. Becoming an effective negotiator is not a matter of playing a win-lose game and coming out on top but rather is about having an attitude of enlightened self-interest and knowing that unless both partners feel good about the outcome, the result is not successful.

Success means more than getting what we want. It's about fulfilling desires with an outcome that leaves both partners feeling good about themselves, each other, and the end result. While this may seem like an unattainable goal, trust us—it's not.

12.

Terms of engagement

With most couples, it's not a matter of "if" there will be another argument but "when." Whether we call it an argument, a difference of opinion, a conflict, a quarrel, a row, a misunderstanding, or a squabble, almost all couples have them. And those that say they don't are either in denial, lying, or exceptionally evolved. Some couples are so emotionally intelligent and mature that they rarely, if ever, experience conflict with each other. The other 99.9 percent at least occasionally have to contend with differences in preferences, personalities, sexual desire levels, taste in movies, food, or politics, as well as in numerous other aspects of life in which couples do not share common values or predispositions.

For most 99.9-percenters, resolving or attempting to resolve differences often involves some degree of struggle. There are, however, some guidelines to help avoid or minimize the defensive patterns that can get triggered when emotions get overheated. Following them could even transform a potentially destructive interaction into an interpersonal engagement that will enhance the quality of the relationship.

We're offering an abbreviated list of guidelines that have worked for many of the clients and students with whom we've worked over the years, and for us personally as well. While old habits can be difficult to break, even the most entrenched patterns are breakable if there is a clear intention to do so. Don't underestimate the power of a true partnership when both people are aligned with the same purpose.

While it does take two to repair a breakdown, it only takes one to initiate the repair process. This is by no means a complete list of all of the possible conflict-mitigating practices, so feel free to add your own.

- State your intention and create agreement before launching into a grievance.
- Be respectfully honest, but not brutally so.
- Specify what's off-limits: for example, violence, either physical or verbal; angry touch; throwing or breaking things; excessive shouting; or name-calling.
- Use time-outs when things begin to get overheated. Either person, at any time, has the authority to call a time-out, no questions asked. All time-outs should have an agreed-upon time to reengage.
- Make requests rather than commands or demands.
- Stay focused on the issue at hand before addressing other concerns.
- Speak about how you feel and what you need rather than what you dislike about the other person.
- Speak from your own experience using "I" statements rather than accusatory "you" statements.
- Keep in mind that acknowledging the legitimacy of another person's perspective is not equivalent to agreeing that they are right.
- Avoid manipulation and excessive coercion.
- Don't issue threats or ultimatums.
- Don't use divorce as a threat in the midst of an argument. If you must discuss it, bring it up when cooler heads prevail.
- Include alternatives when expressing complaints.
- Slow down, pause, and reflect to choose your words carefully rather than blurt things out you might later be sorry for.
- Resist the temptation to give advice unless it is explicitly solicited, and even then, be careful. Keep in mind that providing advice when it has been requested does not require the requester to accept the advice.

- Replace the word *but* with *and*.
- Avoid comparisons between someone else and your partner, like "You're just like your mother."
- Don't punish with silence.
- Avoid using absolutes and accusations like "you always" or "you never."
- Don't interrupt. Apologize when you do.
- Don't invoke the words of others in your defense by saying things like "All our friends agree with me."
- Apologize when you have remorse for something you've done or said.
- Listen without contesting your partner's words. After they have spoken, you'll have your chance to state your perspective.
- At the end of the conversation, thank your partner for making the effort to join you in working towards a successful resolution of your differences.

Keep in mind that this is just a starter kit that can be modified in accordance with the concerns of each partner. There will be setbacks despite your best efforts. Try to be patient with the process and forgiving of your partner and yourself when glitches occur. Hang in there and "go for the gold!"

13.

Control freaks

You know them. You deal with them every day. You may be married to one. You may even be one. They are the dreaded . . . control freaks!

Actually, a more accurate pronoun to use than *they* is *we* since, like it or not, humans are all members of the same clan. *We* all want to control our environment, our relationships, our experience, and our world. We all have our ways of trying to manage our lives in order to promote safety, pleasure, and happiness, and minimize or eliminate danger and suffering. Some control overtly, using obvious means of manipulation like intimidation, issuing threats, making demands, pleading, and nonstop talking. Others use less obvious, more covert tactics, such as passive aggressiveness, going silent, accommodation, withdrawal, flattery, and helplessness.

The drive to maximize pleasure and minimize pain is inherent to the human condition and is operative in various forms and to varying degrees in all of us. There is nothing shameful about having a predisposition towards these inclinations. There are, however, a great many strategies for acting out these impulses, some of which are more skillful than others. The reality is that life involves experiences that bring both suffering and pleasure, some of which are anticipated, some not. We use the word *luck*, good or bad, to characterize experiences to which we can't link causal factors. But in truth, even those situations we think have been caused by our efforts aren't necessarily a result of the factors that we hold responsible.

There's an old story about a man sitting on a park bench, shredding newspapers and tossing the pieces over his left shoulder. A policeman who has been watching him approaches after several minutes and asks him why he's doing what he's doing.

"This keeps away the lions," the man replies.

"Lions?" said the officer. "The closest lions are thousands of miles from here."

"I know," said the man. "See? It works!"

Like the man in the story, many believe that it is because of our efforts to make things go in accordance with our desires that they turn out the way they do. We gather "evidence" that validates our belief that we are in control and which keeps us safe and happy. As long as we can keep the lions away by doing what we think is necessary, we will get what we want and avoid what we don't want.

In reality, our so-called "control" is actually a belief promoted by the illusion of control. In the domain of relationships, controlling behaviors, both overt and covert, not only fail to provide the security that we crave but also serve to perpetuate and even amplify the insecurity that we seek to eliminate. Many of us carry this attitude throughout our lives. When we are possessed by this notion, it's difficult to recognize that this belief isn't grounded in reality. Consequently, we keep reaffirming this thinking and become addicted to reinforcing it by whatever means necessary.

Until we can break free from our addiction to controlling behaviors, meaningful connection in our relationship remains an extremely unlikely possibility. True intimacy depends upon both partners feeling safe, trusted, trusting, accepted, and cherished. These feelings are all incompatible with the emotions generated when we suspect that our partner has another agenda. Operating from an intention to control rather than an intention to connect prevents us from having the kind of experience that we most deeply desire. Until we are willing to risk the kind of vulnerability that deep connection requires, our controlling behaviors will impede our ability to be fully available to others.

Yet despite the conscious desire to be more open and less

controlling, most of us tend to be run by our history. This doesn't mean that we are doomed to forever be at the mercy of overwhelming behavioral patterns, but it does mean that the process of becoming free from our past will likely take more time, energy, and patience than we think it should. Despite our best efforts, we can't "just get over it." Grievances expressed by our partner can activate an impulse to control, particularly if we hold the belief that we are responsible for our partner's feelings and vice-versa. We may believe that the security of our place in the relationship depends upon our ability to adequately provide for their desires. In such cases, hearing our partner's concerns can create anxiety within us, which can activate an impulse to invalidate their feelings. Anything that provokes anxiety in us can promote controlling behaviors.

In confronting these defensive patterns, we shift the focus of our attention away from our partner and towards ourselves, which enables us to try to control something that we actually do have the power to control: our own reactive impulses towards defensiveness.

People control because they are scared. It feels safer to do something, anything, rather than just sit there feeling helpless. It is by standing strong on the only solid ground in our life that we will find the courage true vulnerability requires. That ground is the truth of our own experience. Only when we are willing to defy the impulse to control that gets activated in a threatening situation can we disarm the controller within ourselves. In so doing, our partner's need to control will in all likelihood significantly diminish. And at that point, it's a whole new ball game.

14.
Having a conversation about having a conversation

Linda: I had to learn this one the hard way. In the early years of my relationship with Charlie, whenever there was something I felt we needed to discuss, I would just launch into it, often before Charlie had any sense of what was going on. He never knew what hit him. To put it mildly, this wasn't the best way to initiate a conversation. While I was just trying to be honest about my feelings, Charlie often felt like he had been broadsided by a truck.

The result was that I was now dealing not only with the initial disturbance that had motivated me to speak, but also with Charlie's (understandable) defensiveness. Over time (more than I care to admit), I came to realize that Charlie was interpreting my gestures to heal a rift between us as a surprise attack, which didn't exactly predispose him to being conciliatory. I didn't want him to feel that way. But I had no models from my past for how to initiate important conversations in a respectful way. I was completely unaware of how crucial it is to set the stage for an important dialogue.

Preparation is a neglected aspect of skillful communication. When I did finally come to realize how important this was, I referred to this phenomenon as "introductory remarks." I might, for example, say something like, "I have something that I'd like to discuss with you. Is this a good time for us to talk?" or "I have something that is bothering me. It's touchy material and I want you to know that the reason I'm bringing it up is because I want us to be closer to each other." Or "I want to get something off my heart. I don't want anything to be a barrier between us. Are you available now?"

The main thing I wanted to communicate before initiating the actual conversation was that my intention was to enhance the quality of our relationship and not to criticize Charlie. I wanted to reassure him that I was extending an invitation to a dialogue, as opposed to making a demand, and that I would respect his response to it, whatever it was. Fortunately, Charlie was usually likely to accept my invitation because I was generally willing to take no for an answer if he wasn't ready to talk. By inviting him to choose the time of our talk, I gave him a chance to prepare himself and affirmed his authority as well as mine to influence the process.

All too often a couple will launch into a heated topic before they have properly set the stage. They've already gotten off on the wrong foot. The same anxious feelings that sent them diving into the conversation are likely to have them blurting out statements that are less than constructive. By taking the time to set the stage, one optimizes the likelihood of creating the best possible outcome from the dialogue. Taking a contemplative pause supports a spirit of goodwill and an intention of mutual satisfaction.

I gained confidence when I announced my intention as one of deepening our connection, rather than making Charlie wrong for something he may have done or said. My purpose was to provide him with reassurance. At the same time, I reaffirmed my right to speak my truth, thereby living down a lifelong pattern of pushing down feelings of pain, disappointment, or anger. I reassured myself that I was not simply whining or being mean-spirited. I trusted my desire to create a loving, cooperative relationship, one that wouldn't require either one of us to be subordinate and that allowed both of us to express our needs and desires without fear of reactivity.

Old habits don't die easily, but with work and over time, they do eventually dissolve. Along the way, we get to cultivate other necessary qualities, like perseverance, commitment, trust, integrity, and generosity, that serve us not only in our relationship but in all areas of our life.

15.

When hope isn't enough

Nasrudin was a mythical figure, a teacher from the Sufi tradition. One day, one of his students found him reaching into a bag of hot chili peppers and eating them one at a time. There were tears streaming down his face, his nose was running, and his lips were swollen and irritated. He was obviously in great pain.

"Why don't you stop eating those hot peppers?" the student asked.

"I keep hoping to find a sweet one," Nasrudin replied.

Like Nasrudin, many of us have found ourselves in painful situations in which we continually hope that things will improve soon, somehow. The definition of insanity, according to some people, is continuing the same behavior and hoping for a different outcome. Like the song says, "Wishin' and hopin'" probably isn't going to be enough. Take, for example, the case of Mathew and Julia.

Mathew wasn't a bad guy. He possessed some fine qualities. He was hardworking, honest, a good provider, didn't smoke or drink, and he was dedicated to his family. But as the years went by, his wife, Julia, found herself becoming progressively more unhappy. She felt that something important was missing from their marriage. Whenever Julia brought up a subject she wanted to address, if Mathew didn't want to talk about it, he refused to engage in the conversation. More often than not, he would simply say, "I don't want to talk about it." If pressed, he would tell Julia, "That's just the way I am," meaning "My personality doesn't incline me to engage in those kinds of conversations." What concerned Julia most of all was Mathew's lack of motivation to become a better communicator. Mathew used his conversation stoppers to justify his choices, have Julia accept him the way he was, and get her off his back.

Some of the subjects Julia wanted to discuss with Mathew were very personal: their infrequent sexual contact and his disregard for his personal hygiene. He often neglected to brush his teeth, and his bad breath was offensive to Julia. Mathew also had body odor because he didn't shower regularly. He often dropped his dirty clothes on the floors of various rooms and didn't bother to pick them up. Julia's attempts to bring these issues to his attention were usually met with "You knew this about me when you married me," as if to say she had been forewarned and should just shut up and live with it.

When Julia informed Mathew that she had found a couples' counselor to help them discuss their communication difficulties, he said, "I don't believe in marriage counseling." Eventually it became increasingly obvious to Julia that he had no interest in reconsidering his refusal to join her in discussions that were important to her.

Julia attempted to rationalize her unhappiness by repeatedly reminding herself of all of Mathew's positive qualities. She considered the possibility that her expectations of Mathew were unrealistically high and that she should lower them. Despite her efforts, she was unable to adjust to what felt like a painfully distant relationship and eventually reached the point where she could no longer tolerate the situation. She admitted to herself that Mathew's problem wasn't an inability to change but an unwillingness to accommodate her needs and desires. Finally, unable to continue to make excuses for her husband, Julia filed for divorce.

When I (Linda) spoke to her following the divorce, Julia said to me, "You know, Mathew was right. He was pretty closed mouthed and closed minded when we dated and when we got married. I just didn't want to see it. For years, I hoped that he would change. I thought that my love would be enough to motivate him to open his heart. I realize now how blind I was to his dark side. It's not as if he prevented me from seeing him clearly. I just didn't want to see his shortcomings. I was such a romantic back then. I believed that love conquers all. I'm wiser now and have learned the hard way what I must have in my life. I feel hopeful for my next serious relationship because I know what really matters the most to me. I'm not willing to live without it, regardless of whatever else I'm getting from my partner."

There is a big difference between being patient, with realistic expectations, and tolerating conditions that don't support one's self-respect and needs for emotional intimacy. It was years into her marriage before Julia could tell the difference. She blamed herself for her dissatisfaction rather than recognize her husband's contribution to the condition of their marriage. Her willingness to assume an excessive amount of responsibility for the marriage played into Mathew's unwillingness to hold up his end. It wasn't until Julia recognized that she had been in denial about her pain and how fixed in his ways Mathew was that she could finally extricate herself from her distressing situation.

As grief-stricken as Julia was about the loss of her marriage, she was sadder about losing the happily-ever-after dream she had been cherishing with Mathew. She went on to create a better life for herself and found a partner who joined her in her desire to create a truly meaningful and mutually fulfilling relationship.

Many couples who divorce give up without giving the marriage their best shot. Some, on the other hand, stay in relationships beyond the point where their partner has made it clear they have no intention to make any accommodations to the aggrieved spouse's desires. The optimistic partner lives in hope, believing that their love will eventually bring their significant other around. At some point, like the song says, "You've gotta know when to hold 'em and when to fold 'em." Not all relationships can or should be saved. Knowing if and when to make that call is critical. The truth is sometimes painful to hear but ultimately much less painful than it is to keep eating those hot peppers in the hopes of finding a sweet one.

16.

The shortest complete sentence in the English language

T he shortest complete sentence in the English language is only one word, and it has just two letters. The failure to communicate this word is the cause of as many relationship problems as the overuse of it. That's right. It's *no*. So, how can the nonuse, misuse, or overuse of such a small word result in so many relationship problems? Why is it that so many of us are afraid to speak it when we need to? And why is it that many of us don't say no when we "feel" no?

To find answers to these questions, we need to look at what this word means in the context of relationships. *No* is a refusal to accept something. It affirms a boundary between ourselves and someone who is looking for something from us. It means that we are unwilling to accommodate another's implicit or explicit desires, which risks a reaction that could be unpleasant. Given the preference that most of us have to hearing "Yes," there is likely to be disappointment or even anger if we refuse to accommodate another.

If we prefer not to risk provoking negative feelings in another, we will be predisposed to accommodate their requests, even when doing so goes against our own needs or desires. The problem is that in trying to prevent them from feeling upset, we are not only being dishonest with our partner but also communicating to them that we are willing to do whatever they are asking of us.

Reinforcing their hope that we will fulfill this and other desires can set up an expectation for the future. When one partner comes to expect their desires to be fulfilled and the other is unwilling to use the *n*-word, the likelihood of resentment on both sides increases. If I am in the habit of saying yes when I mean no, I will eventually resent the person who I feel is making selfish demands of me. The truth is that I am choosing to make the sacrifice in order to prevent the possibility of activating his or her anger or disappointment.

Sometimes it may be necessary to risk letting someone down in order to preserve our own integrity. Although we can't always prevent feelings of disappointment or anger from arising, we can respectfully decline to accommodate others' expectations by using responses such as "I'm sorry, but that doesn't work for me," or "I won't be available to drive you to the airport," or "I feel uncomfortable delivering your message to this person, and I'd rather not do it." Or "I can appreciate that you would like me to handle this, but it doesn't feel right for me to do this."

It's a good idea to forgo personal preferences in favor of our partner's. Great relationships always involve some degree of give and take on both sides. It only becomes problematic when the motivation for doing so is to prevent disappointment rather than based upon a genuine desire to give. Bringing more truthfulness into our partnership isn't easy and it can feel risky. But if done with sensitivity and respect, it can make a profound difference. If we can't give an honest no to someone, we can't give a wholehearted yes.

17.

There's two sides to every story

The turning point in most couples' therapy occurs when one or both partners recognize that it's not entirely the other person's fault when a breakdown occurs between them. Every breakdown is the result of contributions both partners have made in creating the circumstances in which they currently find themselves. While most of us would agree that this may be the case, acknowledging this to ourselves and our partner can be a different matter altogether.

There is something comforting in holding our partner responsible, which enables us to affirm ourselves as the innocent party who has been victimized by the offenses of another. Viewing things from this perspective allows us to be relieved of any blame that we otherwise might have to carry. At times, it seems obvious that our partner is the villain. What is also undeniably true is our perspectives are biased by our own subjectivity. Consequently, neither of us has an accurate and complete understanding of the situation. And chances are that we both believe that our view is the correct one and that we have been unfairly victimized by the other.

As a result, we likely see it as our job to enlighten the other person about the "reality" of the situation. As many of us have learned from our own experience, this is a set-up for disaster. Fortunately, this set-up *can* be interrupted, and when it is, the relationship transforms from one that is adversarial to one that is a true partnership.

Brenda and Francisco's real-life experience provides a powerful example of how one couple was able to successfully transition into a mutually fulfilling relationship from one in which they both felt themselves to be victims of the other. Brenda is a woman with a sharp tongue. She has no qualms about speaking her mind and takes pride in her willingness to "let it all hang out." "What you see is what you get" is the way she characterizes the kind of person she is. Her husband of eleven years, Francisco, is soft-spoken and conflict-avoidant. "We're almost total opposites in every way," is how he compares their personalities. When Francisco finds himself on the receiving end of Brenda's judgments, his tendency is to withdraw into silence, which pours gasoline onto Brenda's fire. They didn't argue because Francisco refused to engage with Brenda when he felt attacked, which further infuriated her.

It was Francisco who finally decided that he could no longer live in the cold war that they had co-created. He dreaded the idea of having to deal with Brenda when he spoke with her about his hurt feelings. "I knew that she would get angry at me. Although I was shaking in my boots, and my voice was quivering when we sat down to have 'the talk,' I knew I had to do it, even if it meant getting hammered by her or possibly losing our marriage. I couldn't go on this way any longer."

When they met to talk, Francisco brought some notes with him because he wanted to make sure that he covered all of the points. He thanked Brenda for accepting his request to talk and reassured her that he would like to hear her response after he was done. Brenda paused and then agreed. Francisco opened the conversation with vulnerability rather than hostility and began by apologizing to Brenda.

"I want to apologize for being dishonest with you by not letting you know how upset and hurt I've been by many of the things you've said about, and to me, over the years. I wish I had been more honest with you, and I'm sorry that I wasn't." He then went on to be more specific about the things Brenda had said to him and how angry and hurt he felt and how that caused him to withdraw from her, to protect himself from further attacks. He even admitted that he got some pleasure in seeing how much it upset her for him to go silent.

True to her word, Brenda resisted the temptation to react to Francesco or interrupt him while he was speaking. When Francesco was finished, he thanked Brenda for hearing him out. He added, "I should have said this a long time ago. Maybe if I had, these past few years would have been very different."

Brenda expressed amazement at what she had just heard.

"I had no idea that you had those feelings. When you didn't respond to me, I just assumed that you weren't feeling anything. 'That's Francisco. He's just a stone wall. Nothing gets to him.' Sometimes I would amp up my anger, trying to get at least some kind of reaction from you. At other times, I just walked away with my feelings of frustration and disgust. I had no idea what was going on with you. I just figured that I had a cold, unfeeling husband who did have some qualities that I really liked. I didn't want to lose you, but I didn't know what to do. I just resigned myself to trying to be okay with the package, but underneath my anger I felt lonely and disappointed."

Although this conversation didn't immediately end the pattern Brenda and Francesco had created, it set a precedent that enabled them both to see how they each had contributed to the situation. They recognized that each of them felt like victims of the other, and that each of them bore some responsibility for their circumstances.

In accepting our share of the responsibility for a breakdown, we redirect the focus of our concern away from our partner and towards ourselves, which greatly diminishes the level of defensiveness and hostility between us. In addition, in our willingness to be responsible and vulnerable, we enhance our own level of self-respect and integrity. Bringing this degree of authenticity can feel risky, even dangerous, but like anything that has value, there are challenges that must be met to achieve our intended outcome. When we want that outcome more than we want to avoid the fear of taking the necessary risks, the choice makes itself. When the so-called "victim" sees that they have options other than just resigning themselves to being in what looks like a disadvantaged role, it becomes possible to get honest and then to negotiate for their needs. At this point the system will inevitably shift, one way or another.

There is no way to guarantee that things will turn out the way that we hope they will, and that is why it feels like a risk to see ourselves as co-conspirators, rather than victims. But there is a guarantee that seeing and doing our part will ultimately benefit ourselves as well as the relationship. And we all get to make that choice!

18.

Extroverts and introverts

Darnell is a quiet kind of guy with a great sense of humor. He enjoys getting together with friends, but not too many at once since he's uncomfortable in large groups. He doesn't dislike people, but his tolerance for being around them is somewhat limited, and when he maxes out, he's done, and then he disappears.

Aisha is a high school English teacher and a real firecracker. She's loud, energetic, fun loving, opinionated, outspoken, and she's a big-time talker. And she's married to Darnell.

You'd think that a pair like that would be a match made somewhere other than in heaven, and you'd be right. Darnell and Aisha have been married for sixteen years, and things have been, shall we say, intense. A typical introvert, Darnell tends to seek solitude and time for introspection when his battery needs recharging. When he's under stress, he values no one's company more than his own and finds clarity in being solitary. He's not a loner, and once Darnell is refueled, he's ready to reengage with other people, but not until then.

Aisha, on the other hand, gets recharged by being with people. When she's stressed out, her initial impulse is to get with people, preferably in person, but if that's not possible, then at least by phone. Emails and texts don't do it. She wants real contact.

Aisha: "I fell in love with Darnell because we had such a great connection. We used to talk for hours about the most personal and meaningful things in our lives. I loved his depth and his capacity for listening and understanding; I thought that it would last forever. Boy, was I wrong. I don't know what happened, but over time he became increasingly more distant and less emotionally available. The harder I tried to express my frustration and my need for closeness, the more he withdrew. I thought about divorce, but I cling to the hope that he might change to being the old Darnell that I fell in love with. I know he's still in there somewhere, but I just don't know how to reach him and bring him out."

Darnell has his own version of the story.

Darnell: "When I met Aisha, I was in a very down place in my life. Gloria, my girlfriend of four years, and I had recently broken up. Not surprisingly, she had some of the same complaints about me that Aisha has. 'He's detached, distant, aloof and withheld.' She used to tell me all the time how frustrating it was to be with someone who didn't share himself and spent so much time isolated. It wasn't that I didn't like Gloria; I really did, but she was just too much for me. What was to her a reasonable expectation of connection time was overwhelming to me.

"I wasn't surprised when Gloria called our relationship off. I really did love her and was hoping that somehow things would work out. I wasn't hurting that much until after she left. Then I fell apart. The hole in my life that she had filled was empty again, and I took a dive emotionally. I went into a deep depression and started wondering whether there might be something really wrong with me. What kind of a jerk pushes away a woman that he loves without even making an effort to get her back? I swore to myself that if I were ever fortunate enough to find someone that I loved and loved me, I wouldn't make that same mistake again.

"So, when Aisha and I met, we both fell hard for each other, and I was grateful to have another chance to do it right. The first year we were together was incredible. It didn't take any effort on my part to choose to spend time with her. I loved being back in a relationship. I thought that feeling would never end.

"But it did. Shortly after our first anniversary, I started feeling some of those old urges to seek out more alone time. It didn't happen overnight, it was a gradual process, but Aisha noticed it right away.

And when she did, she tried to reengage me by turning the heat up, and I started feeling really pressured. Needless to say, this didn't help. Things just got worse. The harder she pushed, the more I withdrew. She thought that I was punishing her, but I wasn't. I felt like I was running for my life.

"We got into a vicious cycle that didn't let up, until as a last-ditch effort, we got into marriage counseling. That was the turning point. We're not completely out of the woods yet, but we're on our way, and we both have learned a lot more about ourselves and each other in the process."

Introverts (like Darnell) and extroverts (like Aisha) have opposite—we prefer to call it "complementary"—ways of dealing with stress and meeting their emotional needs. Introverts tend to be self-reflective and seek out spaces where they can access their inner life freely. Extroverts, on the other hand, are predisposed to seek out others with whom they can engage and find the answers to their questions in dialogue. It might seem counterintuitive for these two very different personality types to get together, but it actually makes perfect sense from a relationship standpoint.

If we pair with a partner whose predisposition is the same as ours, the relationship would be unbalanced. Two extroverts would run the risk of burning out without sufficient downtime for rest and reflection. Things could also get heated between the two of them as their tendencies run the risk of overloading their systems, possibly amplifying rather than reducing their stress level.

The potential danger with two introverts is pretty obvious: insufficient external stimulation. The net result of this is that the passion level could flatline. More marriages die as a result of neglect than unresolved differences, so a two-introvert relationship carries its own set of risks as well.

This does not by any means suggest that marriages shared by two similar types are doomed. We have known many couples in two-introvert or two-extrovert marriages who are ecstatically happy. All relationships have their unique challenges, and the predispositions that both partners bring are not the most important variable in the process. The great challenge of all partnerships is to commit to the fulfillment of the needs of one's partner without neglecting one's own needs in the process.

Both introverts and extroverts are challenged to reframe their view of their partner. As this process evolves, appreciation for what one's partner brings that enriches both of their lives replaces criticism, and acceptance replaces judgment. It does take work, and it does take time, but as countless couples know from experience, the payoffs more than justify the effort.

19.

Opposites and complements

Doesn't it seem a cruel joke of nature that most of us find ourselves attracted to people very unlike ourselves? Wouldn't it be simpler if we were drawn to personalities more like our own rather than those that seem like polar opposites? Most of us have an inclination to see our way of viewing things as the "correct" way, and consequently often attempt to persuade others to see things the way we do or to become more like us.

Consider the possibility that these seemingly problematic differences may actually be the very things that add spice to our relationship. We are drawn to others out of needs that are unfulfilled, such as a desire to experience connection, security, love, support, and comfort. On the other hand, some unfulfilled longings have to do with experiences, like adventure, freedom, risk, challenge, and intensity. While these needs may appear to be mutually exclusive, they not only can coexist but may create a "tension of the opposites" that produces passion.

In an age in which external cultural norms no longer enforce the continuation of long-term partnerships, generating internal motivation is essential to their viability. Motivation comes from the ability of both partners to continue to co-create compelling experiences. While security, safety, and comfort are qualities that characterize all fulfilling relationships, without a balance of excitement, adventure, risk, and some separateness, security becomes boredom, dependability becomes indifference, intimacy becomes claustrophobia, and comfort becomes stagnation. The French view this paradox not as a problem but as something to celebrate. Rather than say "Merde" when this apparent contradiction shows up in a relationship, they say, "Vive la difference!" It's "la difference" that makes relationships dynamic, exciting, and even a little edgy. There is of course a fine line between edgy and frightening, just as there is between security and deadening complacency.

Differences show up in a lot of ways. Opposites—or perhaps more accurately, complements—do attract: introverts and extroverts, morning people and night people, impulsive and planners, steady plodders and adrenaline junkies, spenders and savers, adventure grabbers and security seekers. There's no denying that we are drawn to those who counter some of our inclinations with complementary tendencies. While creating some interesting challenges, these differences are the source of one of the most important aspects in any successful relationship: chemistry. *Chemistry* refers to that mysterious quality that fuels the impulse to connect to another. While the first thing that we become aware of in meeting someone is physical appearance, what determines attractiveness is much more than skin deep. Our inner radar senses that something about being with this person makes us feel more whole, even more alive. It's been said that "I love you" really means "I love what I experience when we are connected."

When that feeling is strong, we will be drawn to the person who is the object of our attraction. If the attraction is mutual, we will find ourselves in a state of infatuation, which, as anyone who has been there knows, can be so intense that it seems that we are possessed. This intensity will continue until the passion cools down, which can be anywhere from a week to a year, or longer. But the fire will not necessarily burn out. At this point, the relationship challenge for both partners is to co-create a balance between edginess and security.

When the level of emotional safety for one or both partners is insufficient, the relationship becomes unstable, and feelings of anxiety are likely to arise. This diminishes the sense of security that is important to sustaining the emotional connection. Similarly, an excessive attachment to security can diminish feelings of passion and excitement. In trying too hard to avoid emotional risk, we may inadvertently cool down the heat by transforming our perception of our partner from a lover to a parent, child, or sibling.

A commitment to continual harmony can be as threatening to the relationship as an excessive amount of risk. Creating this balance involves the ability to hold the tension of opposites. Going too far over to one side or the other is unavoidable. Fortunately, it is possible to put in corrections that can stabilize things. Sometimes we have to risk going too far in order to find out how far we can go. There is no fixed point of permanent balance. This is a dynamic process, and the balance point between the two poles of security and adventure is constantly in flux. Complementary differences can, and often do, stimulate challenges that disturb the equilibrium of a relationship. It depends on whether we view them as problems that need to be solved or opportunities that support growth and the deepening of our connection with each other. Since inner predispositions such as introversion or extraversion are unlikely to change over the course of a lifetime, the opportunistic view seems like the best bet. But that's just our opinion. What's yours?

20.

Projection

Projection is the unconscious transfer of one's own desires or emotions onto another person. We can project our inner struggle onto our partner, who may seem like a demon tormenting us with relentless criticism. When we identify our partner as the source of our misery, our goal is to eliminate their influence. We may accelerate manipulative strategies in hopes of silencing or changing them, but these tactics rarely work. Manipulations fueled by discomfort bring forth similar responses in our partner, and the cycle escalates. In the midst of the stress, it can appear as though our partner is the cause of our suffering. The truth is that they are the trigger that illuminates what is already there. It feels like they are making us feel bad, but in reality we are allowing ourselves to open more fully to feelings that our partner has awakened within us.

Over time these denied feelings can lead to breakdowns, depression, and stress-related illnesses. To the degree that we fail to attend to our inner experience, the overall quality of our life will be reduced. Most people do not recognize the source of this diminishment, so they project blame for their feelings onto others. Those to whom we are most closely related are the most likely to be targeted.

We project our disowned parts onto others, trying to coerce them into believing that our unhappiness is their fault, and that we'll be happier if they are different. Underlying our efforts is the message that we don't accept this person as they are, and they must change in order to qualify for our approval. We are not speaking of unacceptable behaviors such as lying, stealing, or deliberately harming others. We are referring to character traits, feelings, or inner qualities that we deem unacceptable, such as exuberance, shyness, anger, or fear.

As we come to recognize and take back our projections, the tendency to automatically attack or withdraw begins to diminish. The ability to remain open and connected to ourselves, even in the face of perceived danger, becomes greater. This allows for a kind of response that can defuse conflict through understanding rather than amplify it through resistance. If we can learn to befriend our inner demons, we will be less afraid of them, they will have less power over us, and we won't be so tempted to project them onto others.

A surefire way of uncovering our projections is to identify our strong negative emotions in response to qualities in others. Generally, the stronger our reaction, the more likely it is that this quality we resist actually exists within us. We can try to go deeper into what we find offensive about this particular characteristic. Often when we inquire into these questions, we discover that fear, envy, or shame underlies our judgmental reactions. Taking back our projections is possible and necessary if we are to find peace within ourselves and with others.

Nowhere other than in our closest relationships do we have a better opportunity to do this work because it is there that our strongest needs, fears, and desires are revealed. There's no time like the present to take the first step.

21.

Making a molehill out of a mountain

According to relationship expert Dr. John Gottman, marriage counselors are spending way too much time on conflict management with their clients and not nearly enough time helping them to build what he refers to as "the fondness and affection system." In plain speak, that means behaving in ways that promote mutual feelings of love and appreciation.

Gottman claims that couples whose relationships are thriving generally have at least five pleasurable interactions for every not-so-pleasurable one. If only one aspect of their relationship is characterized by unresolved issues and five parts of their relationship are characterized by what's working, the relationship will thrive.

To put it in simple terms, Gottman recommends that couples "do more of what's working." This advice is not meant to promote the denial of difficult issues but rather to avoid a preoccupation with unfinished business, particularly when such attention overshadows the positive aspects of the relationship. Recognizing that circumstances require attention is important, but there are times when the most skillful choice is to redirect attention away from the issue temporarily and address the larger context of the relationship.

Having fun together, sharing pleasurable experiences, and introducing novelty can all revitalize a relationship when the prevailing focus has been on troublesome concerns. While it is easy to see things in terms of polarizing extremes like fantastic or awful, blissful or disastrous, always or never, etc., the truth is that all relationships have their moments, good and not so good. The overall health of the relationship is more about the ratio of good and bad and whether we have the knowledge and the commitment to shift the balance when it needs to change. Sometimes we can see a relationship molehill as something much bigger than it actually is. Viewing it as such can become a self-fulfilling prophecy and bring about our worst fear. At other times, the opposite may be true. When we fail to take our partner's concerns seriously, it's easy to forget that thinking something is true does not necessarily make it so.

By consciously choosing to adopt a view that focuses on our partner's positive aspects, we can shift the ratio of positive to negative interactions. Seeing the big picture allows us to put our partner's imperfections (everyone has them) in proper perspective. Affirming that which is working in the relationship and remembering the positive attributes of our partner will enhance the quality of our connection. Despite our desire to do so, none of us possesses the power to change another person. But we do have the power to change the vantage point from which we view them and our current situation, and that can make all the difference in the world!

22.

Are you complete?

In case you're wondering, this question is not about your body parts or whether you have fulfilled your purpose on the earth. Completion is the experience of feeling at peace within ourselves and with others. Some people call it finishing unfinished business. Being incomplete stems from a failure to address differences that have been put on the back burner in the hopes that they would disappear. Generally speaking, they don't. This is the "out of sight, out of mind" syndrome. Unresolved difference can be put out of mind, at least our conscious mind, but if we haven't resolved a conflict, that which is unfinished will have an impact on our peace of mind, whether we are consciously aware of it or not.

Incompletions can manifest in a variety of ways, including physical symptoms such as headaches, heart palpitations, panic attacks, insomnia, backaches, low energy, obsessive thinking, anxiety, irritability, depression, or hypersensitivity. While many people refer to incompletion as occurring between people, it actually occurs within a person. It's possible that one person could be disturbed by a conversation, while the other feels fine. Although it's tempting to make an interpretation that the undisturbed party is insensitive, this isn't always the case. And neither is it necessarily the case that one person is overly sensitive.

We all have varying degrees of tolerance for criticism. We may speculate about the intentions behind the words of others. What's perceived by someone as a personal insult may have been intended by the speaker as a playful remark. Many people use the phrase "Just kidding" to excuse a sarcastic comment that has been hurtful to the person on the receiving end. If we are the recipient of a hurtful comment but don't acknowledge our reaction to the speaker, this may create an incompletion. If we do acknowledge feeling hurt but the speaker makes no effort to respond in a way that leaves us feeling understood, there will almost certainly be an incompletion.

If both parties are willing to listen nondefensively and speak without blame, a sense of connection can be restored quickly, sometimes with just one brief conversation. Listening and speaking without judgment, particularly when emotions are involved, can be difficult for even the most skilled communicators. With practice, however, anyone can master the art of nonreactive listening. Given the prevalence of incompletions, there is no shortage of opportunities to practice!

The presence of incompletions is an indication of the following:

- A failure to understand what is required to come to terms with the issue

or

- A failure to recognize the cost of ignoring unfinished business

or

- A failure to appreciate the benefits of successfully handling incompletions

or

- A failure to trust in oneself or another to engage in the resolution process

or

- A belief that the problem will just go away

Or any combination of the above

These conditions will diminish our intention to confront the issues. Motivation is the key to doing the work. Without a sufficient amount of it, there is little likelihood of resolution. When these conditions are no longer present, the commitment will become stronger. Success in the cleanup process strengthens confidence and motivation to confront incomplete issues rather than ignore them. It's never too late to complete what is unfinished!

23.

How to finish unfinished business

In the previous chapter, we wrote about incompletions and the power of getting complete. Here are some specific guidelines that can facilitate this process:

- Begin by announcing your intended outcome for the conversation you want to have—for example, "My hope in having this conversation is for both of us to feel greater trust and understanding." Or "I feel some distance between us, and I would like to feel closer."
- Reassure your partner that you are not trying to blame or punish them.
- Reframe with the use of "we" rather than a "you."
- Provide your partner guidance as to how they can best support you in this process, such as "It would be helpful to me if you can just let me explain to you what I'm feeling without interrupting me. I don't feel that I've been successful at making my concerns clear in the past, and I'd like to try again. When I'm done, I'd like to hear your response, and I'll do my best to understand you."
- Express your feelings, needs, and concerns, and make any requests that you would like your partner to respond to. If your partner becomes defensive or interrupts you, ask if they can let you finish, and state that you'll be able to be much more open to what they say after you feel that they have heard you.

- Show your partner the same respect you've asked them to give you by listening attentively, not just to their words but also to the feelings that underlie them.
- Resist the temptation to correct them if they say anything you disagree with. There will be time for this later. Keep in mind that not disagreeing with someone does not necessarily mean that you agree with them.
- Go back and forth until you reach a point at which it feels that the energy between the two of you has lightened and you both are more relaxed.
- At the end of the dialogue, regardless of the outcome, thank your partner for joining you in your commitment to deepen the quality of trust and understanding in the relationship.

An incompletion doesn't have to be absolutely resolved in order to create a positive outcome. Some incompletions require many conversations before they become reconciled to the satisfaction of both partners. If you hit an impasse, rather than trying to push through it, take a break and agree to resume at another time. Many of us are very sensitive to criticism. The less defensive and reactive we can be, the more open our partner is likely to be. Becoming more skilled in the process of getting complete is a great way to break the habit of avoidance, and it is one of the best things that we can do for our relationship. There is a learning curve to the process, but it doesn't take a genius to master it. It might be easier than you think!

24.

Reframing

When we feel frustrated or disappointed, it's easy to slip into a negative state of mind. We can have thoughts like "Relationships shouldn't have to be this hard," or "I've gotten involved with the wrong person," or "I'm just not cut out for relationships." Although these thoughts can feel true, they're probably not. If we play these same thoughts over and over in our mind, they become more believable. By the same token, we can replace them with more responsible thoughts, like "I wonder if I have something to do with these breakdowns we keep having?" or "I think there must be something important for me to learn here." The above are examples of reframing problems as opportunities rather than as evidence that proves the situation is hopeless.

Reframing is a deliberate shift in a point of view that enables us to interpret the same situation from a different perspective, preferably one in which new possibilities are revealed. One example of reframing is redefining a problem as a challenge. The word *problem* has an oppressive quality to it, while the word *challenge* is enlivening. With a simple word change, our attitude and energy can be affected. When we're engaged in a hostile interchange and our anger is inflamed, we are more likely to emotionally shut down and experience critical thoughts. This can cause us to feel overwhelmed with agitated emotions and render us temporarily helpless. At such times, we are predisposed to demonize the other person and view them as an adversary. In doing so, we increase the likelihood of them reciprocating with the same attitude towards us.

If we can reframe our view that we are being besieged by a dangerous enemy to a perspective that recognizes that we are both possessed by strong emotions, we can de-escalate a negative spiral. This doesn't mean that we bypass our anger; we experience it without reacting from it. Doing so opens the possibility of breaking the vicious cycle that we both have created. Either person can initiate this reframe, and the likelihood of tensions cooling is greatly increased.

A dramatic example of this process comes from Viktor Frankl in his groundbreaking book *Man's Search for Meaning*, where he shares his experience of having been imprisoned in four concentration camps during the Second World War. He lost his beloved wife and all of his family and observed most of his fellow inmates die. Frankl kept his mind active, planning the lectures he would give after his release, using material from the camps to illustrate points he wanted to teach. As a devoted teacher, his careful, deliberate planning of his future lectures kept his spirit and body alive in the midst of unimaginable conditions. He survived the death camps for years and went on to realize his vision of using his experiences to help others heal from their suffering. Hopefully, none of us will ever have to endure the hell of Frankl's life in the concentration camps, but we can use his example to keep our attitude hopeful, even in dire circumstances.

Reframing requires seeing something in a new way, a context that allows us to appreciate previously unrecognized aspects of our situation. At that point, we see whatever life hands us as opportunities rather than problems. Breakdowns can be transformed into challenges that offer new possibilities. By practicing the art of conscious reframing, we can come to trust that our ordeals can be redemptive and even produce growth.

We can come to appreciate the potentially transformative power of conscious suffering and learn, as the spiritual teacher Stephen Levine refers to as the challenges of "keeping our heart open in hell." The deeper the channels pain carves, the greater our capacity for joy. We will uncover inner resources we didn't know we had. And best of all, we get to share our hard-earned wisdom with others, not only those in our inner circle but everyone whom we touch, even briefly.

25.
The downside of "doing what comes naturally"

Charlie: Several years ago, I attended a lecture by a well-known spiritual teacher and arrived late, which was not an unusual occurrence for me in those days. His talk had been going on for about twenty minutes, and on my way in I asked the doorman if he could give me a condensed version of what I'd missed. He paused for a moment, then said two words: "Trust yourself." I sat in for the rest of the talk, which was commentary on the theme of self-trust. Not so much about what it actually meant, or how to develop it, but examples of how powerful self-trust is and what a difference it can make in my life when I have it.

At the end of the talk I had some thoughts about self-trust. In any given situation, there are multiple selves offering their opinions about possible actions to take. Which self should I trust? Which is the "real me"? Is it the one urging me to take the risk or the one that wants to play it safe? Is it the one that tells me to go ahead and indulge my desire for a second helping of pasta or the one that admonishes me to resist the temptation? Is it the one telling me that it's okay to exaggerate the amount of time I work out each week or the one that tells me to be totally honest? I knew (or at least believed) that I had a "true self" and that I had an ego and that I sometimes had trouble distinguishing between the two.

Over time, I've learned to discern who is talking, although even these days there are times when I'm not exactly certain. One of the things I have learned is that what feels familiar isn't necessarily my "truth," and what feels uncomfortable isn't necessarily untrustworthy.

When it comes to relationships, the tendency to favor the familiar is strong, and the voice that suggests anything other than that seems incorrect. Doing what doesn't come naturally is sometimes the very thing that can neutralize habituated patterns that no longer serve us.

Here are some examples of things we can do to interrupt habituated patterns:

- Go on a "blame fast." Resist the temptation to focus on what the other person has done wrong and take responsibility for your contribution to the breakdown that has occurred, blaming neither yourself nor your partner.
- Try to resist the temptation to withdraw from uncomfortable feelings, and instead bring an attitude of curiosity and interest to investigate what you are experiencing and why. While some interactions can be painful, the willingness to feel the truth of your experience can provide you with the understanding you need in order to connect more authentically with your partner. More often than not, denying the reality of your experience in the long run causes much more suffering than facing it does.
- If you feel discouraged, reaffirm your commitment and remember why this relationship matters to you.
- If your best efforts fail to bring about your intended outcome, enlist support from others (family, friends, and professionals).

This last point is a big one. Many of us resist asking for help out of a belief that we shouldn't need it. There is no such thing as an entirely self-made man or woman. No one has ever achieved success in anything without support and assistance. Once we free ourselves of the myth of independence, we are more than halfway there!

26.

The ultimate danger sport

It's probably safe to say that most committed partnerships are formed out of high hopes and the expectation that each of us would be happier with our partner than without them. Otherwise, why bother? The trouble starts when the relationship inevitably moves out of the infatuation stage. The root of the word *infatuation* means "foolish" or "deluded." Infatuation is nature's way of tricking humans in order to perpetuate the species. The "trick" is to get us to believe that what we see, think, and feel is the "truth" about who this person with whom we have fallen in love really is. It's a state of temporary delusion, inevitably followed by another stage commonly known as that of "disillusion," which is characterized by a concern that we may have been mistaken in our initial impression of our mate.

There is great variation in the length of the infatuation stage. It can last anywhere from a few days to several years. We know a couple who has been married for nearly seventy years who claim to have never left the state of adoration. Other couples have told us that they saw the underside of their partner on the first date but chose to get married anyway. Since everyone has an underside (often referred to as the "shadow"), trying to eliminate from eligibility those who fall short of our ideal would result in a pretty solitary life.

We are on our best behavior when we're first attracted to someone, attempting to create the most favorable impression and concealing aspects of our personality that others might find unattractive. Meanwhile, the other person is probably doing the same thing.

After a while this game is likely to become tiring. Disillusionment is frequently a two-way street. If our partner isn't the person we thought they were, then it's pretty likely that we aren't the person they thought we were either. Some blame their partner for deliberately misrepresenting themselves. Some blame themselves for not being the person they believe they "should" be. Some decide that the institution of marriage itself is a bad and unnatural idea. And a small number see their difficulties as a valuable learning opportunity. The last group fares much better in the long run, which raises the question of why some people choose to see relationship challenges as opportunities to develop inner qualities, strengths, and skills, while others see them through very different eyes.

Whether we see ourself as a victim (of poor parenting, fate, bad luck, an unloving partner, etc.) or a responsible agent in the determination of our destiny depends on our perspective. Those who have lived from the perspective of the victim will be more inclined to see the world through darker lenses, and to feel ineffectual, hopeless, helpless, resentful, and pessimistic. Reaffirming this worldview provides "evidence" that it's futile and naïve to even try to alter what looks inevitable. The "benefit" in adopting a victim stance is that it offers a perfect justification to avoid behaviors that may be risky or require significant effort. The downside of this stance is that it promotes a deeply embedded sense of powerlessness in one's life.

The alternative to assuming a victim stance is the adoption of the view of life as a series of learning opportunities. Doing so will almost certainly confront us with defensive patterns that have been reinforced in our thinking for years, if not decades. This is the place where the rubber meets the road. Changing embedded habits is no easy task and requires a strong commitment to overcome an attachment to a tried and true orientation. It is possible, however, with support, effort, practice, and intentionality, to replace outmoded views and defensive strategies with life-affirming perspectives. And when we do, we can find ourselves living in a different world.

In choosing this perspective, the focus of our attention moves from the other person's behavior to our own present experience. Rather than getting stuck on what they are doing wrong, we look instead at what we can do to move things in a more positive direction. It's not about coercion; it's about revealing rather than concealing, connecting rather than protecting, expressing rather than repressing, and accepting rather than rejecting. It also means exercising an appropriate level of discernment when setting boundaries, and being responsible for taking care of ourselves by not tolerating disrespectful behavior from others. As we practice, over time old patterns lose their grip on us, and we become increasingly liberated from their control.

The path of committed partnership is fraught with peril, and the stakes are high. Two of our most cherished desires are on the line: being connected to others and being free and autonomous in our own life. For this reason, we refer to committed partnership as "the ultimate danger sport." This game is not for the faint of heart. If you're up for it and have found a partner who shares that intention with you, you are most fortunate. And so are they.

27.

Schismogenesis

Schismogenesis. It's a term that you're not likely to have heard very often, unless you're studying esoteric words for a spelling bee or are a graduate student or researcher in anthropology. It was coined in 1935 by Gregory Bateson, who was married to Margaret Mead, and together they were two of the most highly regarded anthropologists of the twentieth century. Bateson used the word to refer to unskillful forms of social behavior between individuals and groups. In his book *Steps to an Ecology of Mind*, he defines schismogenesis as a "creation of division."

The term derives from the Greek word *skhisma*, or cleft, a division into opposing factions. Bateson's hope was that researchers would discover methods that allow one or both parties to stop escalating cycles of misunderstandings, reactivity, and breakdowns in communication before things reach the destructive stage. Over eighty years later, therapists, marriage counselors, researchers, and the general public are still searching for how to deal with interpersonal differences in a way that enhances relationships rather than damages them.

If, for example, a couple is engaged in a conversation that has become adversarial, there is no point in continuing the dialogue when schismogenesis has shifted things into the destructive zone. When tensions increase beyond the point of clear thinking and nondefensive responding, a mutually satisfying outcome isn't possible unless a de-escalation occurs. Often, just a few moments of quiet can cool things down. But in cases of extreme emotional arousal, a longer time-out is necessary in order to regain composure.

Interrupting the downward spiral, however, isn't always enough to break the cycle. Another factor often needs to be in place in order to effectively reengage in a meaningful way. That factor is intention. When steamed-up couples use their break time to nurse their resentment, they are reinforcing rather than diminishing their angry feelings, which will continue to amplify tensions. Unless the break time is used with an intention to soothe each person's inflamed emotional state, the desired outcome of a deeper mutual understanding will in all likelihood not occur.

How we soothe ourselves during the pause can be the determining factor in the process of de-escalation. It is important to not use this time to brace ourselves against our "opponent." Such a view predisposes us to view the other person as an adversary rather than as a partner.

An effective way to promote reconciliation is to focus our attention on thoughts that promote compassion, hopefulness, and gratitude towards our partner. For example, we might want to remind ourselves that we have gone through difficult interactions in the past and successfully restored goodwill. Or we can tell ourselves, "I am lucky to have a partner who will continue to engage with me about tough subjects, who is willing to hang in there even when things get heated, and who won't give up on me." This kind of self-talk admittedly isn't easy to do, particularly when your mind is inflamed with fear, anger, or hurt, but it can transform a heated debate into a productive dialogue.

Creating our own self-soothing stories can help us avoid schismogenesis and the slippery slope from disappointment to hostility. The ability to do this skillfully is one thing that distinguishes couples who fall into the pit of despair from those who manage to stay out of it. These stories help us to regain our composure, which allows us to reengage in a nondefensive rather than an adversarial way with our partner.

While this doesn't guarantee that the other person will join us in a stance of openness, it makes this outcome much more likely. Just as defensiveness begets more defensiveness, so does openness invite a reciprocal response.

Recognizing the possibility of reconciling even the most difficult of relationship impasses and knowing what that process entails can provide the motivation to practice our new skills. As we cultivate the self-discipline needed to move towards greater interpersonal harmony, feelings of distress dissipate, and our competence and confidence grow. This can be a turning point that deescalates tensions and liberates us to delight in our cooperative connection.

28.

The high cost of winning an argument

One of the widely held myths that threaten relationships is the idea that being victorious in an argument is a good thing. That notion is based in part on the assumption that there are only two possible outcomes to arguments: winning or losing. It's a zero-sum game, and if we don't come out on top, there's only one other place we can go. Given this mindset, it's no surprise that so many people embroiled in a conflict use amplified threats, insults, and various forms of character assassination. "You're just like your mother!" "No wonder your last wife left you!" "You're the most selfish person I've ever known!" "I can't take this anymore. I'm calling a lawyer tomorrow!" And these are just the mild ones!

Then there are the more subtle forms of coercion and manipulation, designed to discredit the other person's position or to invalidate their concerns. While there are infinite strategies for winning an argument, only a few motives drive this intention. The most prevalent one is the desire to avoid an anticipated humiliation, punishment, or loss of power by defeating the other person and, in so doing, affirming a dominant position in the relationship.

When the trust level is low, both partners are likely to feel a strong need to be concerned with the degree of power and control they possess since they are vulnerable to abuse, exploitation, or domination. The buildup of defenses and aggressive behaviors is not an effective deterrent to attack, nor does it repair damaged trust. On the contrary, it adds to the problem and often provokes further hostility.

Consequently, trying to "win" an argument by defeating the other person not only fails to address the underlying problem, but it also intensifies it. While one person may appear to win the battle, both of them lose the war. When it comes to committed relationships, when one person loses in the short run, they both lose in the long run. When someone loses or gives up in resignation, trust goes down.

Even though the active fighting may end, the underlying issues have not been adequately addressed, nor have the differences been resolved. When this is the case, the spirit of cooperation is broken, and both partners begin to see each other as adversaries rather than teammates. Vulnerability is then replaced with defensiveness, interrupting the flow of honest communication, and each person becomes more concerned with personal protection than the establishment of a mutually satisfying outcome. This diminishes the feelings of goodwill necessary in order to reestablish trust and shared respect.

At this point both partners are operating from misaligned personal intentions, and each of them sees the other as a threat to their well-being. Fear rather than love has become the dominant motivator on both sides. Even when one person seems to be more angry than frightened, in fact both are experiencing fear but may be enacting different protective strategies (such as aggression and withdrawal or intimidation and accommodation). When arguments fail to address the underlying issue that has been activated, the real concerns will likely go underground. Although this creates a temporary pause in the hostilities, it is not a permanent fix.

When we try to settle differences by winning the argument, we lose the opportunity to find mutual understanding. While not all relationships are "made in heaven," a lot more of them have the potential to become heavenly than we may think. If we are willing to challenge and interrupt embedded defensive patterns that may be doing more harm than good, the outcome can exceed our greatest expectations.

29.

The real deal about deal-breakers

One of the most frequently asked questions from our readers and students is "What are the deal-breakers in relationships?" Deal-breakers are those behaviors or conditions that one partner is unwilling to tolerate. Because *tolerance* is a relative term subject to everyone's capacity to accept varying degrees of distress, there is no one-size-fits-all answer to this question. There is no higher authority that we can defer to that legitimatizes or negates our right to refuse to tolerate a specific behavior on the part of our partner.

While one person may be willing to tolerate occasional affairs, another may be unwilling to stay together after a single betrayal. The same goes for physical or verbal abuse, or addiction, or chronic dishonesty, or different religious beliefs. This is not to say that we shouldn't make an effort to work out the different values all couples have in regard to their beliefs, attitudes, and behaviors. What can push a situation from the workable to the unworkable zone is an unwillingness to confront the situation honestly and directly.

A willingness on the part of the "offending" partner to consider altering his or her beliefs or behaviors is required in order to create a deeper level of trust and understanding. If an alcoholic has no motivation to modify his drinking habits or a parent is not willing to discuss her child-rearing philosophies respectfully with her spouse, the chances of that situation becoming a deal-breaker are greatly increased.

In cases of behavior that is destructive to self and/or others, such as any form of abuse or addiction, the key element is the degree to which the addict or abuser is committed to their own process of recovery. If there is lack of commitment to changing one's behavior, the relationship is unlikely to be sustainable. On the other hand, even a serious addiction can be overcome and eventually broken if the commitment is strong.

Yet even in cases where both partners are willing to make their best efforts to work towards the resolution of a divisive issue, it may not be possible to prevent the situation from falling into the deal-breaker category. The longer an unacceptable condition is tolerated in a relationship, the more likely it is to become toxic. A toxic relationship is one in which the level of trust, respect, and goodwill has deteriorated to the point where the motivation to heal the partnership has been lost.

Couples take serious risks by accepting circumstances that cause extreme suffering. Living in unrealistic hope or denial only causes greater suffering in situations that may be inherently intolerable. While facing the truth can be difficult, in the long run, it is the most direct path out of suffering.

While there is no way (nor is it necessary) to assess what percentage of the problem is due to each person, generally both partners have perceptual filters that prevent them from seeing the full range of options available to them. This is where help from a trusted friend or professional can illuminate possibilities that may have gone unrecognized.

The earlier we respond to entrenched relationship differences, the more likely it is that they will not deteriorate to the point of becoming deal-breakers. Still, sometimes despite our best efforts, we can be faced with true deal-breakers. In cases where it is clear that fundamental differences are too great to bridge the gap, it is wise to acknowledge this reality, create a respectful end to the relationship in its present form, and move on.

Commitment doesn't necessarily mean that we stay together forever, no matter what, but that we stay engaged in the process of

88 AN END TO ARGUING

honoring one another as best we can. Sometimes the best thing we can do is to try to become more accepting of our partner or their behavior. But at times, the best way to express our love is by refusing to tolerate something in another that is causing harm.

Not all relationships can or should be saved. Knowing and trusting our limits and needs is an essential condition for any relationship. Every committed partnership deserves our best shot. When that fails to fulfill our stated intention, it might be time to consider plan B.

30.
Differences are inevitable; conflict is optional.

Opening the possibility of avoiding arguments in the face of differing viewpoints has to do with whether the intention of either person is to dominate or to create mutual understanding,. Arguments can be minimized or avoided if one of the partners is committed to reconciliation. Here are some guidelines that will help to create a conversation that can lead to a mutually satisfying outcome.

What such a result requires is willingness to . . .

- Have your intention include a satisfying outcome for both partners and communicate it to the other person. For example: "My hope is that each of us will hear and understand each other's perspective so that out of the dialogue a greater understanding can be reached."
- Listen without contesting the content of the other's words. There will be time for that later.
- Paraphrase what you heard. Restate, in your own words, your understanding of what you just heard. Paraphrase as many times as you need to until your partner feels that you've got it right.
- After an understanding is established, thank your partner and ask if they are interested in hearing your side of things. If they say no, let them know how you feel in regard to this conversation.

- Resist the temptation to criticize your partner, and keep your focus on what you feel and need.

If your partner states something you disagree with, let them complete their conversation, and when you do respond, don't try to persuade them to see how that position is incorrect, but rather express your point of view. When a conversation is contextualized as a quest for understanding, the tone often shifts from being combative to being conciliatory. Even when one partner insists upon identifying a winner and loser, it is possible for the other to refuse to argue, simply by acknowledging the position that is being put forth and stating their perspective without coercive efforts to secure agreement. It often helps to offer the option to simply gather information from each other without needing to determine who is right and who is wrong.

The key element has to do with the willingness of the person who desires a nonadversarial dialogue to drop any manipulative maneuvers. This form of emotional openness requires the willingness to risk vulnerability and to resist the temptation to become defensive even if things become more heated.

If this stance can be held in the face of strong emotions (admittedly, no easy thing to do), the other partner's attachment to their position will likely soften. This allows for a deeper understanding of the unspoken fears and concerns underlying the positions each partner has taken.

In cases where an adversarial partner is repeatedly unresponsive to the vulnerability offered by the other, it may be unwise to continue the conversation. At this point it's helpful to acknowledge, without blame, an impasse that for the time being seems impenetrable, and to suggest that the conversation be resumed at another agreed-upon time. The chances for productivity are increased after both partners have had an opportunity to cool down and revisit the subject with an enhanced level of receptivity. If the adversarial partner refuses to disengage, even temporarily, the other is compelled to separate as respectfully as possible.

Arguments can be avoided, and when we consider the futility of trying to resolve differences by efforts that are coercive, controlling, and manipulative, the motivation to learn more effective ways of dealing with differences can grow exponentially. As we become "conscious combatants" rather than angry adversaries, we become increasingly skillful in the art of respectfully engaging with another while simultaneously holding our own ground and honoring our truth.

31.

Preventing differences from turning into conflicts

rguments are like snowflakes; each one is unique. Even when couples tell us that they always have the same argument, we usually notice small, sometimes microscopic differences in their words, body language, and tone of voice. These differences aren't due to the details of the argument—who never takes out the trash or spent too much money shopping—but are caused by each partner's emotional activation. That's the one thing all these arguments have in common: they are about something other than the difference that has precipitated the conflict.

The precipitating incident is the gateway to figuring out the underlying concerns that need to be addressed. Conflict is usually driven by one or more of these factors: feeling threatened, anxious, hurt, unloved, or unappreciated; fearing the loss of love; or experiencing an unhealed childhood wound that has been triggered.

Focusing on the details of the argument rather than the emotions behind it is a distraction from the recovery process. This diversion inevitably hijacks the process of resolution and leads to further misunderstanding. Recognizing that we are off track enables us to make a correction and get back on course. With practice, couples can avoid the pitfalls of ineffective strategies altogether.

Here are a few guidelines for staying on track and practicing what we refer to as "conscious combat":

- Be honest. As obvious as this may be, many find it easy to excuse "white lies" or other forms of dishonesty, such as exaggeration, fibbing, telling half-truths, or euphemisms. The bottom line is that an intention to mislead is a form of dishonesty.

- Don't name-call or characterize your partner in negative terms. If unkind words slip out of your mouth during an argument, apologize as soon as you become aware of what you've said and take responsibility by communicating what you were feeling beneath your anger (hint: fear or hurt). If your partner calls you names, try to resist the temptation to retaliate by doing the same.

- Create an agreement with your partner that neither of you will make any physical contact with the other when either of you is in a state of anger. Wait until tempers have cooled down before you touch each other.

- Don't throw things at people, walls, or anywhere. Verbal expressions of anger are fine unless they are intended to wound or punish the other person rather than to clear emotions that have been withheld and are inhibiting your ability to be open.

- Avoid making threats or delivering ultimatums. There's a big difference between saying something like "I'm so frustrated that I could scream" and threatening divorce. While divorce may be a legitimate option, the time to discuss that it is not in the heat of an argument.

- Speak without blame or judgment; blaming and judging will only put your partner on the defensive.

- Use time-outs. Create an agreement that permits either partner to call a time-out when they feel a burst of anger. Both partners should have the authority to call a time-out when they feel it's needed.

- Communicate your feelings and needs rather than your opinions, judgments, and assessments.

- Offer advice only when it's solicited, and even then, be careful.

- Slow down. When speaking, take time to pause and reflect. Resisting the urge to speed through your communication will make it easier to stay in touch with your feelings and minimize the likelihood of blurting out words that you might later regret.
- Remember to show appreciation. Thanking your partner at the end of the interaction, even if you haven't resolved the issue, helps to promote goodwill and openheartedness, two of the most important qualities in any relationship.

The things we've talked about here are the basics. Following these guidelines doesn't guarantee that differences won't turn into conflict. However, doing so will make it more likely that we'll remain focused even if we get that sinking feeling of "Here we go again." Even the best relationships have their moments. By putting into practice these guidelines and those in other chapters, we can minimize the likelihood of breakdowns.

The art of navigating relationship challenges is crafted over time and begins with a shared intention. There are no shortcuts, and there will inevitably be moments of frustration and disappointment, but with the practices outlined in this chapter, these moments will happen less often and be less intense. Anything worthwhile in life has both costs and benefits. When it comes to relationships, the benefits far outweigh the costs. Give it a try. You might be very pleasantly surprised!

32.

Holding the tension of the opposites

We've all found ourselves in this position a time or two in our lives: A decision needs to be made, and we're of "two minds" in the matter, meaning we see compelling reasons for choosing either one. But in choosing, we may lose potential benefits or experience negative consequences of either one. The pros and cons of each side seem to neutralize each other, which makes satisfying both desires seem impossible. What to do?

This dilemma shows up in myriad forms in all relationships. It is epitomized in the Clash's hit song from the '80s "Should I Stay or Should I Go?" This tune repeatedly poses a question that we ask ourselves when we are confused as to whether to remain in a relationship that has obvious positive aspects and equally obvious not-so-positive aspects.

The condition of "being of two minds" doesn't just relate to the matter of continuing or ending a relationship. It can come up in less consequential matters, such as "Should I let the other person have their way or take a stand for what I want?" or "Should I tell her the truth and risk hurting her feelings?" or "Should I tell her what I think she wants to hear?" There are many other possible examples.

The most important aspect of these polarizing situations is not the question we're asking but rather to whom we are directing the question. When faced with what seems like impossibly conflicting factors, most of us are prone to seek advice from others, who are usually willing to provide their opinions. More often than not, their advice, well intended as it may be, won't provide us the relief we seek.

The person who needs to get clear about the answer to this question is the one asking it. That would be ourselves. But what do we do if we've been trying to answer the question and have failed to come up with a response that seems adequate? Doing nothing gives us a break from the quest to find "the correct answer." Actually, we *are* doing something. We're doing what the title of this chapter encourages us to do: holding the tension of the opposites. Holding two contradictory options is very different from trying to decide what to do.

Sometimes the best thing to do in the midst of a frustrating dilemma is to give ourselves permission to take a break and drop into a deeper level of understanding. Making excessive efforts can be the biggest obstacle to finding clarity. When we can clarify our thinking, it becomes much easier to recognize possibilities that are invisible to us when we are scrambling to answer the either/or question.

Loose ends can create anxiety, but while it is true that resolving incompletions sooner rather than later is always a good idea, there are times when taking a break best expedites the process. Sometimes resisting the urge to do something can be our best response to a perplexing situation. In that place of "nondoing," clarity often comes when we least expect it.

33.

Confirmation bias

L ife requires us to make assessments. We assess risk level, costs, benefits, and appropriateness of behaviors in specific situations. We make these judgment calls in our relationships, too, but sometimes forget that they are subjective evaluations and therefore hold our views as being objectively true. Taking a position in this way is a form of judgmentalism and can be hazardous to the health of our relationship. It also sets us up for conflict since a fixed position invites a counter position.

Being judgmental can be disastrous because once we attach to a fixed characterization, it becomes very difficult to see things (or people) differently. Attachment to a judgment prevents us from accepting new information that may conflict with our current view, leaving us unable to update assessments that are no longer accurate. Most of us tend to seek out information consciously and unconsciously and make interpretations that reinforce established views. This process is known as "confirmation bias," and everyone does it.

Paul discovered this the hard way. He had been self-centered, insensitive, and controlling in his relationship with his wife, Cookie. When Cookie announced that she was no longer willing to tolerate his disrespect, he apologized and promised to mend his ways. Shaken by her remarks, he committed to be the loving husband he had promised to be in his wedding vows. His resolution was to become an ideal life partner and to focus on doing what he believed would make Cookie happy. He immersed himself in self-help books, workshops, and therapy. He brought Cookie flowers, expressed interest in how she spent her days, and stopped expecting her to wait on him. He shut off the TV and listened to her when she wanted to speak with him. But no matter what he did, Cookie continued to view him through the lens of her preestablished perspective.

It was as if she had taken a snapshot of Paul years ago and put it in the photo album. She couldn't turn the page and still had it open to the same old picture. Cookie laid in wait for evidence that proved Paul was untrustworthy. Since no one is perfect, Cookie easily managed to collect "evidence" that Paul was guilty of deception. She held a zero-tolerance policy and was unwilling to forgive Paul or to give him the benefit of the doubt when he slipped, even briefly, into old patterns. She was convinced that Paul's past had disqualified him from any second chances. She claimed that her motto was "Fool me once, shame on you. Fool me twice, shame on me."

Despite his resolution, Paul eventually began to feel like there wasn't any point in continuing to make the effort since, in her mind, he was guilty until proven innocent. He concluded that he had no control over how she viewed him. Cookie's attachment to her judgments prevented her from appreciating the changes in Paul. Reestablishing trust after it's been broken takes time, and while Paul had given Cookie reason to mistrust him, Cookie played a part in the deterioration of their marriage. Her relentless focus on Paul's past prevented her from recognizing her role in the breakdown.

When Paul eventually told Cookie that he would no longer try to prove his love, she took this as more "proof" that he had been pretending all along. Shortly thereafter, Paul decided that his best efforts were insufficient to persuade Cookie to see him as being sincere in his love for her. Cookie's attachments to her judgments did shield her from the pain of a potential future disappointment, but that protection ultimately caused the dissolution of their marriage.

But Cookie was not the only one in the marriage who was guilty of judgmentalism. Paul had previously judged her as being unworthy of the respect she had asked for. Unfortunately, the shift in Paul's attitude toward Cookie came too late. She was already possessed by confirmation bias.

As of our last contact with them, Paul is remarried and claims to have learned his lesson. Cookie remains single with no intention of marrying again. "I'm not bitter," she told us, "just clear that I don't need to be married to be happy. I'm doing fine, thank you." Still, you have to wonder.

34.

Why you shouldn't pick your battles

Charlie: Over the years, I have heard and used the admonition "Pick your battles" quite a few times. It's even been one of my most frequent pieces of advice. The phrase suggests that every relationship has an abundance of topics on which couples have differing perspectives and that it's a good idea to be selective in regard to which ones are worth fighting over. Those different views can show up in a variety of situations, ranging from relatively benign decisions such as choosing a restaurant or movie to choices over where to invest savings and which religion to raise the children in. "Picking your battles" has to do with the idea that it's neither reasonable nor productive to argue over every little thing.

Stating a preference isn't the same as trying to coerce our partner to agree with our view or trying to manipulate them to take actions that will support our desired outcome. Some things are of course worth taking a stand for, but not everything. The key is in being able to discern the difference. Doing that can spare us and our partner a lot of unnecessary suffering. The process of making that distinction begins with how we frame the situation in our mind. The words that we use to define it, whether they are unspoken thoughts or are expressed aloud, have a great deal of power to set the context for the type of communication that ensues.

Conceptualizing an encounter as a "battle" predisposes each of us to assume an adversarial position, since battles result in winners and losers, and the stakes can be high. Realizing the hazards of adopting such an orientation often isn't enough to bring a "win-win" intention to the conversation. Even the term *win-win* suggests a contest that involves opposition. It's not possible to agree on everything. The point here is to recognize that the conversation starts before any words are spoken. It begins with the intention with which we enter the dialogue and the language that we use to characterize it.

Choosing whether or not and how to take a stand as opposed to choosing a battle creates a greater likelihood that what follows will be a respectful dialogue rather than an antagonistic struggle. There's a difference between taking a position and taking a stand. To take a stand is to express a perspective strongly without judgments, ultimatums, threats, or unsolicited advice, unlike a position which often includes one or more of them. Taking a stand doesn't necessarily require a strident voice. In fact, it is more likely that the other person will hear us if we have done the preparatory work to present our point of view with clarity rather than volume. Self-reflection allows us to speak with a quiet dignity that predisposes others to be more receptive to our message.

When we see an exchange as a battle to be won or lost, our focus is on the other person. We want to find their areas of weakness, to deliver strikes designed to diminish the ability of their will to prevail over us. This view invariably generates a counterreaction in them, and by the time the first words are spoken, we've already transformed differences into conflict. When we're in a battle, it feels safer to focus on the other person, since they represent a threat and we need to be aware of potential dangers.

The notion that the best defense is a good offense applies in contact sports but not so well in the kind of contact that we seek in intimate partnerships. The time to focus on our partner is when they are expressing their perspective. Giving them our full attention to try to understand how they feel and why they feel that way creates an empathic connection that promotes greater openness and trust. It also increases the likelihood that they will respond in kind to our concerns.

Shifting an intention from winning to creating a satisfying outcome for both partners isn't easy, particularly when it comes to things that we have strong preferences about. It doesn't necessarily mean that we have to settle for compromises that leave us both feeling that we didn't get what we needed. While most of the differences couples have are not of the deal-breaking variety, some are genuinely challenging. What is important when faced with one of these situations is to try to remember that the way that we engage in the process has everything to do with its outcome. The way we get there is what we get! A "win at any cost" attitude is unlikely to produce a mutually satisfying outcome, whether we get what we want or not.

When we appreciate the degree to which all relationships are enhanced by breaking the habit of responding to differences with defensive and offensive reactive patterns, we've already taken the most important step in becoming liberated from our automatic, adversarial programming. And that one step is a game-changer!

35.

Emotional intimacy

Setting: Jennifer and Ellen's kitchen on a Sunday morning. They are cleaning up after sharing brunch.

Ellen: Honey, I've been feeling some distance between us lately, and I'd like to talk with you about some of my concerns. I think that both of us have gotten caught up in our jobs, and I've been missing you.

Jennifer: Well, I'm right here. If you want to talk, just let me know.

Ellen: It just seems like the content of our conversations these days focuses on the business of running the household and we don't have time to connect the way we used to. I miss those times.

Jennifer: Well, that's what happens when you get married and have a family, isn't it? You know, the honeymoon ends, and you get on with the work of taking care of business.

Ellen: Just because that happens to a lot of other people doesn't mean that it has to happen with us. I know that it's not inevitable that we have to lose the juice we used to have. Nothing is more important to me than the quality of our connection, and I'm not willing to watch things go downhill without doing something about it.

Jennifer: What do you mean, "go downhill"? Are things that bad between us?

Ellen: They're not exactly "bad," they're just not what I want them to be, what I know they could be. You're right. Our work and other concerns have pushed everything else, including our relationship, into the background, and I've been noticing that lately I've been feeling disappointed in our lack of contact. I'm not blaming you. I'm as caught up in juggling my life as you are yours. I just want to nip this in the bud so that six months or two years down the road, we don't find ourselves in a train wreck.

Jennifer: Well, you picked a hell of a time to drop this on me. You know that Sunday morning is the only time I can really relax. I was just getting ready to watch a movie.

Ellen: That's okay, Jen. We don't have to talk this very minute. I feel better just having spoken to you about how I feel, and I'm glad that you also want to make things between us even better than they already are.

Jennifer: I do.

Ellen: How about if we pick a time in which we can be together without any distractions from the kids or work or the phone or anything else.

Jennifer: (sarcastically) Sure, when, next year?

Ellen: (returning the sarcasm) I think we might be able to find some time before then.

Jennifer: Like when?

Ellen: How about Saturday morning? You don't work on that day, and I can skip my aerobics class at the club. That will give us all morning.

Jennifer: To do what?

Ellen: Whatever we want! That's the idea, Jen. One of the reasons it seems that our lives are all work and no fun is because every minute of every day is scheduled for something. The only way we're going to be able to bring more quality time into our lives is to schedule it.

Jennifer (sarcastically): How romantic. Breakfast at eight, lovemaking at nine, shopping at ten.

Ellen: Come on, Jen. If the only way we can be sure of having open time in which nothing else is going to infringe on us is by scheduling it, and I'm willing to do it. Otherwise, our other responsibilities will just continue to eat up all of our time and energy. Besides, we're not scheduling anything in particular for that time; we're giving ourselves three or four hours in which we can do whatever we feel like doing.

Jennifer: Sounds good. I'm in.

This scenario may have a familiar ring to it, although for many of us, things can easily go off the rails early on in the conversation. This conversation was actually about creating agreement that both partners were committed to. If it seemed that this interaction went unrealistically smooth, let's take a look at some of the reasons why it didn't deteriorate into a shouting match.

One of the reasons things went the way they did was that Ellen consistently spoke in terms of her own desires, and never implicitly or explicitly blamed Jennifer for not fulfilling them. She took responsibility for coming up with a strategy to interrupt the pattern in which she and Jen had become stuck. At no time did she react with hostility.

If she had any judgments, she kept them to herself. She was honest and sensitive to Jennifer, while not walking on eggshells, and she stayed focused on her own concerns without pressuring her partner to accommodate her expectations. Had Ellen gotten critical or reactive at any point, there likely would have been a flare-up resulting in an entirely different outcome. The less frustrated and disappointed we feel, the less likely it is that our attempts to create shared emotional closeness will be experienced as criticism by our partner, and the less likely they will respond defensively. The feeling of emotional safety enhances the chances of meaningful connection.

At least as important as Ellen's words was the tone of voice she used in conveying her concerns. She was serious but not heavy-handed; clear, but not grim; committed but not controlling. Sometimes a couple waits too long to address unfinished business, and when one of them expresses their concerns, it comes out sounding angry because they have been marinating in their feelings for too long. The sooner we address problematic issues, the less likely our communication will be contaminated by buried resentment.

Meaningful connection requires a high level of transparency. Couples who engage in this level of connectivity enjoy a sense of peace within themselves and with each other. They also freely express gratitude towards each other.

All this adds up to a formula for enhanced mutual emotional fulfillment. There are bumps along the road, even in the best of relationships. Seeing the bumps as inevitable makes it easier to not take things too personally, and to communicate nondefensively. And that makes all the difference in the world!

36.
The greatest gift you can give your partner

Charlie: Like many other people, I grew up believing that marriage required self-sacrifice, and lots of it. I thought that successful couples put each other's needs ahead of their own and denied themselves pleasures that weren't compatible with their mate's preferences. It's no small wonder that I wasn't exactly enthusiastic about the prospect of getting married. In the hidden side of my independent, commitment-averse self, however, was the part of me that craved connection, affection, and (let's be honest) regular sex. So, at the age of twenty-five, Linda and I got married, but my feelings were somewhat mixed when we tied the knot.

The biggest challenge for me, particularly in the early days of our relationship, was in deconstructing some of the less-user-friendly beliefs I had brought into marriage. The process turned out to be considerably more demanding than I had anticipated. I am pleased to say that overall, things have met or in many cases exceeded the hopes and expectations I started with. I've succeeded in proving myself wrong in many of the beliefs I inherited from my family and their families before them.

Breaking a chain of beliefs that has been reinforced for generations is a formidable challenge, and although I can't say, "I did it," I can say that I am doing it. I'm delighted to find myself wrong about my belief that someone else's happiness is more important than my own and that it's selfish or uncaring to be happy when a loved one isn't feeling so great.

The greatest amount of support I received in confronting this misguided belief came from Linda, who coincidentally had some of the same misconceptions I did. She helped me to see that I didn't have to become a martyr and sacrifice my own happiness in order to make our marriage work. And she helped me to see that my responsibility in creating a fulfilling life for myself was as important as anything else I could do for her or the kids. "We don't want a husband and a dad who feels unhappy and burdened, no matter how much money you're bringing home." I had to hear that message about 5,000 times before I finally got it!

Fortunately, Linda's got a lot of patience. And perseverance. Over the years, it's become increasingly clear to me that the quality of my life experience is no less important than the quality of anyone else's. If I don't take care of business in my own life, I will inevitably burden others with the obligation to carry that responsibility. It is not Linda's job, or anyone else's, to see to it that my needs are met and that I experience fulfillment in my life. This has probably been the most valuable lesson I've ever learned, and one that I keep relearning at deeper levels.

Most of us come into partnerships looking for what we can get: love, attention, security, pleasure, companionship, as well as distraction from unpleasant feelings or thoughts. When we no longer hold our partner responsible for the fulfillment of our needs and for our happiness, everything changes. It is perhaps the single most important thing we can do to ensure that our relationship will be mutually satisfying.

Taking care of ourselves isn't selfish; it's necessary. Of the multitude of gifts Linda has given me over the course of our over fifty-year history together has been the awareness that the greatest gift I can give her is my own happiness, and for that I will be eternally grateful.

37.
Going for the gusto!

Linda: At the beginning of my relationship with Charlie, what I wanted most in my life was the comfort and security of a committed partnership. I grew up in a family where chaos and struggle ruled, and I was determined not to replay that scenario in my adult life. I hungered for and chose a partner who I believed would provide me with that. To my surprise, that's not the way it went. Our relationship proved to be more conflictual and less peaceful than I expected.

Charlie and I seemed so far apart in our views, desires, and even values that I frequently feared we wouldn't make it. The fact that we did I attribute to hard work, determination, good help, and love. We both had to stretch into each other's world. Over time, Charlie's hard edges gradually softened, and I became more flexible and learned to let go of some rigidly held beliefs and expectations.

The longing for comfort, predictability, and security is inherent in all human beings, although the degree varies from person to person. I tend to play it safe. Charlie tends more towards the risk end of the spectrum. As I would eventually discover, security alone does not a great relationship make. When an extreme degree of rootedness is present in a relationship, we may feel weighted down, cramped, caged, or even suffocated. In addition to roots, we all need wings that enable us to soar.

Many of us opt for predictability rather than risk the instability that can come with change and growth. Unfortunately, an attachment to predictability can, in the long run, squeeze the juice out of a relationship. The quest for eternal security and comfort can lead to boredom, complacency, and ultimately, stagnation. Too much of a good thing becomes a bad thing. Truths are left unsaid, needs repressed, desires denied, all in order to avoid conflict and keep the peace. What felt like security can begin to feel like incarceration.

Many relationships involve each person holding one of these two polarities (adventure or security), and one thing that distinguishes great relationships from good ones is that each partner is able to honor both of these aspects and move fluidly between them. When this is the case, the relationship becomes invigorated with a vitality that promotes co-creativity rather than codependency, and a quality of both relaxation and passion infuses the couple's shared life.

A romantic partnership involves the interplay of many polarities and abilities, including giving and receiving, action and contemplation, feeling and thinking, and separateness and connection. While few of us are equally comfortable with both sides of each duality, we can learn to appreciate the value of our partner's ability to bring into the relationship those tendencies that are less developed in ourselves. While it is likely that our natural tendencies will remain dominant in our predisposition, it is possible to strengthen our less dominant side through practice and by paying attention to our partner and learning from them.

To prevent the stultifying influence of extreme predictability, there needs to be a fullhearted commitment from both partners to deepen the passion and vitality of the relationship. By making the quality of our relationship a high priority, we greatly increase the likelihood of an adequate degree of adventure as well as security for both partners.

There are practices that can enhance the development of this equilibrium and create a greater balance of these two tendencies. Here are a few of them:

- Checking in with each other on a regular and frequent basis
- Practicing self-reflection to maintain awareness of your own

needs and monitoring the degree to which you are fulfilling them
- Expressing both your appreciations as well as your grievances to your partner when you become aware of them and not allowing them to become withholds
- Expressing your love through actions that reflect your gratitude towards each other

Passionate relationships require the willingness to be authentic and respectfully honest in expressing the full range of our emotions. Our challenge is to see our partner through eyes of acceptance and to allow ourselves to be fully seen by them as well. When each of our actions reflect these principles, the excitement of discovery, so enchanting in the earliest phases, can continue and deepen throughout the life of the relationship.

Keeping the mutual appreciation flame burning requires both partners to stay on the path of ongoing growth and discovery. It's never too late to make a different choice, even if our relationship has become stale. There are risks to disturbing the status quo, but they are small compared to the potential benefits. A balance of security and adventure, the familiar and the novel, characterizes relationships that sparkle over the decades. A fierce, loving connection coupled with the freedom to be our unique separate self is a genuine possibility for everyone. It's a lot of work to get all the moving parts humming along, but well worth the effort. Why settle for less?

38.
Enlightened self-interest

Joan: "Frank and I have been married for over thirty years. He was a career diplomat, and I had faithfully followed him to his many posts around the world, being a supportive wife and mother of three. I made deep friendships and started projects wherever we lived, always only to be uprooted by Frank's inevitable transfers. When we finally returned to the United States and our children had matured and were on their own, I decided that it was finally my turn to follow my heart's desire, and I chose to get a graduate degree at the local university. I won a full fellowship. I was ecstatic that it was finally time for me to take my turn.

"Then, just before school started, Frank had a massive heart attack that nearly killed him. On the way to the hospital, I made up my mind to let go of my long-awaited dream of pursuing my education. The next day, when Frank opened his heavily drugged eyes, I said to him, 'Frank, don't worry. I'll stay right here by your side. I'm not going to go to graduate school. That's not important anymore. I'll stay home and take care of you.' I thought that my words would reassure him. I was wrong. Despite the oxygen tubes coming out of his nose, the IV tubes in his arm, the EKG wires running off his chest, and the nurses rushing in to hold him down, Frank managed with a massive effort to heave himself up to a near sitting position. "Joan . . . you will do no such thing. You must go to school . . . you must!' His eyes were huge from the effort, and he was glaring at me. The nurses glared at me too. 'Okay, okay, I'll go to school.'"

Frank: "I spent a month in the hospital, recovering, while Joan went off to start school. I made my experience into a meditation retreat. It was a turning point in my life to let go of my ambition after decades of striving. What Joan sees as a great act of generosity was not a sacrifice but a gift to her, to me, and to our marriage all at the same time."

"Enlightened self-interest" refers to the understanding that what a person does to enhance another's quality of life enhances one's own quality of life to a similar degree. It is the idea that "what goes around comes around." The Buddhists call it Karma. The happiest couples report that they derive great pleasure in giving to each other. While most actions are motivated by a desire to fulfill our own needs, acts of enlightened self-interest serve the well-being of others as well. Everybody wins.

This cycle of mutual generosity creates a self-reinforcing loop that becomes more enriching over time. The most successful couples don't "give to get" in a codependent way but rather give from a well that is already full. These are the kinds of remarks we hear all the time from couples who delight in their relationships:

- "I enjoy doing things that help; that's why I do them."
- "I'm not a particularly unselfish person. I do things that make me feel good, and making her happy is one of my greatest joys."
- "His happiness always comes back to benefit me."

When our partner's fulfillment is a high priority, our personal preferences become subordinate to an intention to give. Feelings of sacrifice dissolve because we are not giving up anything that we really need. Getting "my way" becomes less important because getting "our way" becomes what we really want. To fulfill our desires at the expense of our partner's missing out would leave both partners feeling diminished. We still have our personal preferences, but all they are is preferences. We are more concerned about the fulfillment of a higher purpose, which is the well-being of the relationship. We are finally relieved of the need to keep score, since the object of the game is no longer to make sure that we get our share; it's to co-create as much mutual happiness as we can.

When we begin to make the other's needs as important as—not more than—our own, we are on our way to creating a conflict-free relationship. This is not to say that differences won't occasionally show up, but they will usually show up more as preferences than as attachments that need to be accommodated. In these circumstances, preferential differences are much less likely to turn into painful arguments.

The shadow side of enlightened self-interest is that when our partner feels pain, sadness, or disappointment, we are so strongly connected to them that we too suffer. Feeling our partner's pain is part of the price of sharing the joy of each other's happiness.

Imagine what life would be like if we brought enlightened self-interest into all of our relationships. Consider the possibility that it is the most practical thing we can do. Enlightened self-interest is in everyone's interest.

39.

The power of vulnerability

Linda: Arguments don't end when one person overpowers another. Submission to an intimidator might interrupt the heat of the battle, but at best, it's a temporary truce, not a permanent resolution. Even with a truce, there is generally a not-so-subtle tension present in the relationship because conflict has been driven underground where it continues to fester.

To move towards resolution during times of distress and conflict, it's necessary to experience the one thing we most desire to avoid: vulnerability. The peace of understanding will not come as a result of efforts to get our partner to stop fighting and start listening. It is much more likely to result from the openness that arises out of a willingness to disarm ourselves of our verbal defenses. This requires us to give our partner (who probably looks more like an opponent at this point) the receptivity and honesty that we want them to give to us.

This kind of vulnerability takes trust—not just trusting them not to exploit our nondefensiveness but also trusting ourselves to provide the comfort and support that we will need if we do experience emotional injury in the process. We are challenged to put down our own sword and shield at those times when we may feel most vulnerable to attack. To do so requires us to proceed from an intention to speak from the truth of our current experience and reveal our current feelings, thoughts, concerns, and desires rather than focus on ways in which we can disarm, punish, or coerce our partner into accommodating our demands and seeing things our way.

Years ago, I was in the habit of responding to Charlie's faultfinding and unsolicited advice with counterattacks involving criticism, judgment, and blame. Not surprisingly, he countered my counterattack with counter-counterattacks. And, well, you know how that goes. In no time at all we would find ourselves locked into a closed loop that took us down the proverbial rabbit hole with neither of us feeling accepted, heard, or understood. We were each convinced that we were right and had no interest in hearing the other's take on the "truth." It wasn't until I stopped saying, "You never listen to me" and "You always have to be right" that the impasse between us began to dissolve. At the time, I was convinced that I was just speaking my truth. As it turned out, I really wasn't. What I was actually speaking were my thoughts, opinions, judgments, beliefs, and condemnations.

When I finally saw that doing so was not producing the results I was looking for, I decided to try something else. Instead of lashing out in frustration, I made opening statements like "I really want us to understand each other. It's so painful for me when we don't connect." By revealing my own frustration and pain rather than "correcting" Charlie's responses, the tension between us softened, and we became better able to hear each other.

Personal disarmament is the act of standing undefended and speaking the feelings, usually fear or pain, that underlie our anger. The more I practiced, the less fearful I felt, and the easier it became for me to lower my guard.

Emotional honesty almost always brings forth more of the same from others. Regardless of how our partner responds to us, undefended communication is itself a transformative gift to ourselves as well as to our relationship. In honoring our truth, we deepen the development of self-trust, self-worth, and self-respect, while simultaneously bringing greater honesty and integrity into the relationship. I have learned the most from those who have lived their own advice. When we "walk the talk" and give what we desire to receive, the process becomes its own reward.

Vulnerability provides us direct access to the deeper truth of our own experience. It brings us into greater integrity with who we are.

This level of authenticity connects us to ourselves and creates a safe climate for mutual care and tenderness to blossom. That's a success in and of itself. The gift to our partner is the openhearted access to our underlying feelings of warmth, care, and affection as well as access to their own similar feelings towards us that their anger and fear have obscured from them. I've seen from my own experience how interrupting the cycle of defensiveness can break long-standing destructive argumentative patterns. There's no denying that disarming ourselves can feel like very risky business; but continuing to reinforce the cycle has risks as well. It's up to each of us to decide.

40.

Every accusation is an autobiography.

Brett and Michael represented opposite ends on the spectrum between play and responsibility. In optimal relationships, each partner has both aspects within themselves, with a predisposition to favor one tendency or the other. Things can get dicey when one or both partners demonize the other for being "irresponsible" or "way too serious." Brett and Michael were such a couple. In addition to assessing him as irresponsible, Michael saw Brett as being childish, lazy, immature, and self-indulgent. He did admit to enjoying the playfulness, humor, and fun that Brett so naturally brought into their relationship, without which "things would not be as much fun." Still, Brett's disinclination towards self-discipline and his "poor work ethic" drove Michael crazy on a daily basis, and he wasn't reluctant to remind Brett of his shortcomings.

Brett sometimes was able to hear Michael's complaints without getting defensive, but despite his laid-back nature, Brett had his limits. He had a job, but strife, worry, and stress were not his style. He and Michael argued a great deal about who would do which household tasks. Their arguments never got resolved. Both of them were convinced that they were right. The kernel of truth in each of their views kept them stuck in a painful pattern, each with their heels in cement.

Michael usually brought up his grievances first. "I need more help around this house. You act like such a kid. Where is your ambition? You seem lazy to me, and I can't see how you will ever get anywhere in your life. I feel like the parent around here. Can't you just grow up?"

Brett: "I'm not goofing off; I'm enjoying my life. You are so uptight. Why can't you just chill out?"

The words weren't always the same, but the message was. They both were trying to get the other person to change and become more like they were by raising the ante in the shaming game. It was a recipe for disaster. By the time they decided to get counseling, things had gotten pretty broken down. They were both starting to use the *d*-word.

In counseling sessions, they both cooled down enough to listen to each other and hold their tongues without counterattacking. As they increasingly felt heard, they were each able to look at their own part in the predicament. Michael became aware of feeling overworked. When he began to own up to how he admired Brett's ability to bring playfulness into his life, and how lacking he felt in that area, he began to learn from Brett about responsible self-care. As Michael changed, their relationship changed as well. Rather than continue to see it as "Michael's problem," Brett grew to more fully appreciate Michael's industrious and giving nature.

Judgments or concerns that we have about others often reflect aspects of ourselves that we haven't yet fully accepted. This failure to accept disowned aspects causes us to meet our partner's responses with frustration and judgment rather than with curiosity, understanding, or openness. When Michael saw Brett as a mirror that reflected back to him unacknowledged parts of himself, he became more able to make skillful decisions. He could admit that the overly responsible part of himself had been in control most of his life. He saw that his pushy style had been offensive to family, friends, and coworkers, and had cost him cooperation with others, not just Brett.

As Michael focused more on himself, Brett no longer felt the need to defend against criticism and began to undertake some introspection of his own. In the process, he became more aware of the legitimacy of many of Michael's complaints. He saw that as the only male in a family of five kids, he was accustomed to being treated like a "little prince" who didn't have to grow up because responsibilities were the jobs of others.

They went on to establish a strong working partnership. Brett is still the more playful one, but he now carries what both agree is an increased level of responsibility in the family. Michael learned to take better care of himself, and he has discovered that the world doesn't end when he takes a much-needed break. He has developed a greater appreciation for the value of relaxation, play, and fun. He also has come to realize that when he has a strong emotional response to Brett, there is often some valuable information present for him to discover about himself. They are still in competition with each other, but now the game is about deciding who got the best deal!

41.

Making room for the shadow

The term *shadow*, coined by the psychoanalyst Carl Jung, refers to the unlit side of the personality that lies outside of conscious awareness. It includes those aspects of the heart, mind, and soul with which we have not yet fully come to terms. Qualities and tendencies that we assess as being unacceptable facets of ourselves and threatening to the personal and public image that we cherish are relegated to the shadow. It is the closet into which we banish from public sight everything about ourselves that we fear can diminish others' opinions of us.

Everyone has a shadow. The question isn't whether or not we have one but what is in it and how we relate to it. Most of us have learned to deny the shadow to others whose judgment we fear and to ourselves as well. Since a "shadowectomy" is not possible, the next best option is to accept it so that it ceases to inhibit our ability to live a life of authenticity and integrity. If we fail to do this, we will either project it onto others, internalize it with negative self-judgments, or both. Either way, the result isn't pretty: a life filled with judgments, complaints, condemnation, rejection, and disappointment. The capacity to experience joy, pleasure, and spontaneity is diminished, and authenticity and aliveness are replaced by a desire for control and defensiveness.

Our primary partner, if we have one, is more likely than anyone else in our life to illuminate and activate our shadow and for that reason will in all likelihood be the one with whom we have the most difficult interactions. The good news is that it's when the shadow is activated that we can begin to free ourselves from its grip and bring it into the light. In doing so, we can tap into its hidden gifts that are inaccessible when we are busy keeping it hidden and out of our and others' awareness.

Usually, only after years of struggling to conceal do we realize—after the second divorce, a major depression, a job loss, a heart attack, or some other health crisis—that trying to keep the shadow locked away and out of view is a losing battle.

Ultimately the shadow will have its way with us, revealing itself in ways, and at times, that we least expect. To avoid being surprised when our shadow unexpectedly reveals itself, we can take matters into our own hands. We can "out" ourselves on our own terms, by acknowledging our imperfections and weaknesses. Even in worst-case scenarios, in the end, we will ultimately be better off when we are no longer in the grip of the need to live up to others' expectations. We can finally find the peace that comes from simply being who we are. In so doing, we discover, as John Lydgate famously said, "You can please all of the people some of the time, and some of the people all of the time, but you can't please all of the people all of the time." And that's okay.

42.

Who's in your shadow?

Mary and Doug had been married for twenty-seven years when she was diagnosed at age fifty-two with breast cancer. Virtually overnight, their marriage, which had been characterized by a high degree of trust, respect, and intimacy, became a battleground in which Doug was the object of all of Mary's fear, pain, and rage.

"It was like getting hit by a truck," said Doug. "It just came out of nowhere. One day we were in love with each other, and the next day, it seemed like she wanted to kill me. The cancer diagnosis really threw us both, but I never expected that reaction from Mary. No matter what I did, it seemed like nothing was good enough. Every effort I made left her feeling angrier with me. After a while I just gave her more space, but this infuriated her even more. She raged and accused me of abandoning her. I knew that she was scared; we were both overwhelmed by the cancer, but nothing I did seemed to help. I wasn't going to leave the marriage, but in all the time that we'd been together, I had never felt so close to giving up."

"It was as though I was possessed by a demon," was the way Mary described her experience. "For the first six months after the diagnosis, throughout the chemotherapy, the surgery, and the radiation treatments, I was a raving lunatic. It wasn't just Doug who was the recipient of my wrath; it was everyone, but he got the brunt of it. It wasn't that I hated him; it was that somehow the cancer had ripped open the doors that contained all of the rage I had been stuffing my whole life. Fifty years of being a good girl, a nice person, a patient wife, pretending that I never felt angry or helpless or tired or upset.

"It came up all at once. It seemed like there was no controlling it, and even if I could, part of me didn't want to. Even while I was raging at Doug and feeling guilty about dumping so much on him, a bigger part of me was saying 'Yes! Go for it! It's about time! You've swallowed enough shit for three lifetimes. No more!' I know Doug didn't deserve what I was dumping on him, but I would do the same thing if I had it to do over again. For the first time in my life, it seemed as though I wasn't driven by my fear of displeasing people. What did I have to lose? For the first time, I finally felt free!"

What Mary experienced was a form of what we call "shadow possession." When we fail to honor the unwanted aspects of ourselves for prolonged periods of time, a life crisis can unexpectedly rip the cover off our feelings, exposing us (and others) to the raw emotion covered by a lifetime of denial. All hell breaks loose.

Not only did Doug and Mary's marriage survive their crisis, but they came through it with more personal strength and shared love than they had ever previously experienced. They both describe their current relationship as having greater depth and authenticity than they had prior to her diagnosis. Mary says, "Cancer forced us into a place that we had been avoiding throughout our marriage. It confronted us with the fact that we had been settling for the comfort of denial rather than the passion that comes from real honesty. The first thing we both had to get honest about was how dishonest we had both been. We next had to admit how much more we wanted out of the marriage and how afraid we were of going for it. We had both been playing it safe, and if it wasn't for the cancer, we probably still would be."

Doug: "I can't really say that I'm glad that Mary got sick, but I am grateful for the changes the crisis provoked in our lives. I wouldn't want to go through it again, but what we came through it with was sure worth it."

43.
It's not about finding; it's about digging!

A fable: There was once a rich man who wanted a supply of fresh water on his property, so he decided to have a well dug. He gathered a group of workers to dig on a spot he believed was a likely source of water. At a depth of ten feet, they hit water, but the well went dry in just three days. He chose another spot on the land, and the men began digging. Once again, they hit water at ten feet. This time, however, the water contained sulfur and had an unpleasant odor, so they went to another part of the land and dug another well. Sure enough, they hit water again at ten feet, but the water came in a tiny trickle. The diggers continued to hit obstacles and move to new locations in search of fresh water, but they never did find it. Ironically, the water the man sought would have been available in almost any of the places they had dug if they had simply continued digging. They only needed to go further down.

Many people's concept of relationships is like this story. Because there are so many readily available alternatives, we may feel impatience in our quest to find the right (perfect) partner. Yet as many have come to understand, the path to relationship fulfillment has less to do with who we find (although that is certainly an important factor) than it does with what we discover and cultivate within ourselves in the process of being in our relationship. It can be tempting to seek out another partner when things get difficult. And although the time may come to move on when our best efforts have been unsuccessful, many people give up before they've made their best efforts.

Loving another without losing ourselves is the essential challenge of all committed partnerships. Balancing the commitment to self and other requires ongoing attention and calibration. Some of us find it easy to focus on the needs of others and are adept at giving love but have difficulty receiving it or attending to our own needs. Others are preoccupied with their own desires and tend to be less mindful of the needs of others. Often those with opposite tendencies attract each other. Unable to effectively come to terms with these differences, the initial promise of the relationship may deteriorate into despair or separation. This scenario is common, yet few of us possess the tools necessary to meet this challenge.

The digging that we need to undertake to bring about a fulfilling partnership is an inner digging in which we mine our own depths to discover and uncover the riches within that we may not have previously recognized. Like the man in the story, we are guaranteed to encounter obstacles and impediments, each of which will require us to choose whether to give up or to dig more deeply to find the hidden reserves that enable us to access the true building blocks of relationships, including openheartedness, courage, commitment, vulnerability, honesty, trustworthiness, and compassion.

We are not born with these and other qualities fully developed but rather come into the world with their seeds within us. It's the challenging events of our lives that provoke us to dig deeper. In so doing, we access the inner resources needed for the journey towards wholeness and authentic connection that relationships offer. Just as we need resistance to push against to strengthen our body, we need to encounter resistance in the form of obstacles, challenges, and even ordeals in order to ignite the life force within us. Settling for an unfulfilling relationship takes a toll on our self-esteem and sense of self-worth. We might start to wonder if we are defective and whether this kind of relationship is all we deserve. By continuing to dig deeper, we are choosing to believe that we have the power and self-worth to improve and are deserving of a greater quality of life.

This commitment to the relationship must be coupled with a strong commitment to our personal well-being in order for both partners to flourish. The qualities of self-care, generosity, and enlightened self-interest serve to strengthen both sides of this equation. Care of another can take many forms as well. Showing up in a more meaningful way for our partner, stretching into their world, showing more interest in their life, and learning how to love them in the ways they want to be loved are examples of digging down to the sweet water that nourishes. In engaging in these and other practices, we become less reactive. In focusing on what our partner is rather than what they aren't, we can come to feel more appreciation and less disappointment, which causes affection to flow more freely between us.

According to the late author and philosopher Ken Keyes, "The secret of life is sticking with it." Those of us who have stuck with the process of deepening our partnership know that difficulties are inevitable in relationships. We've heard from a great many couples who have reported that they were tempted to quit when serious breakdowns occurred, but they chose to hang in there despite feeling discouraged. The path of committed partnership is by no means the path of least resistance, but for those who have a taste for the *real* good life, it can be the fast track to our destination!

44.

Stuffers and shouters

Bella was a pleaser, going way out of her way to present herself as being a nice person.. Her life was dedicated to smiling, being positive, and trying to keep her wife, Fay, happy. Fay was a pistol. She had a fiery temper, and she didn't believe in repressing her emotions, particularly her anger. On more than one occasion, she let Bella (and others) know "I don't believe in stuffing my feelings." Fay's mother died of ovarian cancer before she was fifty, and Fay was convinced that her illness was caused by silently suffering at the hands of her husband's relentless physical and emotional abuse. Her mother was passive and quietly tolerated her husband's cruelty, keeping her feelings from everyone but Fay, with whom she often commiserated. Fay decided as a small child that no man was ever going to mistreat her.

Fay knew that Bella was distinctly different from her father and that she would not treat her disrespectfully. Yet despite Bella's efforts to accommodate her, Fay managed to find things that displeased her and which she continually brought to Bella's attention.

Bella was at her wit's end. "No matter how hard I try, it seems that my efforts are never good enough. Fay always finds something about what I'm doing or saying that isn't acceptable to her. I generally just try to accept her criticism because when I argue with her, she rages, and I'm no match for her. I don't have the stamina to go toe to toe with her. It seems to make more sense to me to withdraw, which enrages her even more. I'm at a loss over what to do."

Although Bella wasn't expressive of her feelings, repressed

emotions have a way of leaking out in the form of broken promises, sarcasm, "forgotten" agreements, unsolicited criticism, and other forms of passive-aggressive behaviors. Unacknowledged resentments and fears will almost always get expressed one way or another, even if they never come out directly. The result of these leaks in their relationship was that Fay's feelings of frustration were amplified, which drove Bella further into her corner and fueled her reactivity. Bella and Fay downplayed the toll this pattern was taking on their relationship as well as on their personal well-being. It wasn't until they both became concerned that their marriage was in real danger of dissolving that they finally decided to get some professional help. During that process, they were each able to recognize the part they had played in the crisis and were able to interrupt the cycle of blame, accommodation, and withdrawal.

They recognized that each of them was driven by very similar fears and that they both were afraid of conflict and had different strategies for dealing with it. Bella tried to accommodate Fay, but her efforts failed because Fay wanted her to engage rather than to acquiesce. Fay's method of avoiding conflict was to intimidate her partner, whom she saw as an opponent, and disarm her with threats.

Because many of us associate responsibility with fault and blame, we go to great lengths to avoid punishment. Doing so can bring about disastrous results. As Fay and Bella each came to accept the underlying feelings driving their behaviors, their impulses towards aggression (passive or active) gradually diminished, and they became more willing to be vulnerable with each other. The vicious cycle was interrupted, allowing for more respectful interactions.

We see many versions of this dynamic in our work with couples in which one partner passively accommodates and withdraws and the other acts as an angry intimidator. In nearly all cases, each one sees the other as the guilty party and themselves as being the innocent victim. In truth, neither is completely guilty or innocent, but rather they are both (usually unconscious) collaborators who have co-created a system that enables them to reenact their defensive patterns.

We have never found a case in which one partner is solely responsible for a relationship breakdown. Although both partners play a role in interpersonal breakdowns, it's not necessarily fifty-fifty. It isn't necessary, or even possible, to determine the exact percentage of responsibility each person has. What matters is that each understands that they have contributed to the situation in which they currently find themselves, and recognizes what they can do to repair the damage. This does not occur overnight, but with practice, right intention, and effective support, even the most damaged partnerships can be transformed into a mutually respectful relationship. Yes, it does take work. And yes, it does take time, and yes, it is doable. And well worth the effort!

45.

Authenticity

"He who dares not offend cannot be honest."

—Thomas Paine

One main factor that sets great relationships apart from merely good ones is the depth of emotional intimacy. Other factors contribute, but authenticity, vulnerability, and deep emotional connectedness are right at the top of the list. When two people commit to diving into themselves, they become, in the words of our friend Sam Keen, "psychonauts," who—unlike astronauts, who explore the outer reaches of space—choose to explore the inner reaches of the heart and mind.

Creating deep emotional intimacy is not for the faint of heart. Like other explorations of new frontiers, it requires courage, motivation, and a spirit of adventure. When a life lacks authentic interpersonal connection, it begins to feel dry, flat, dull, and superficial. An underlying sense of anxiety and/or depression is the price that we pay when we are more committed to avoiding upsets than to interacting with authenticity. Resurrecting the passion for living requires not only a desire to be aware of our emotions but also a willingness to reveal them to others. Fortunately, tolerance is possible even for those who tend to be judgmental by cultivating acceptance, understanding, and appreciation.

Couples who enjoy high levels of satisfaction are not necessarily the ones who have the least conflict but rather those willing to relate with honesty and sensitivity. They have developed communication skills that enable them to deal respectfully with their interpersonal differences. They are, to quote psychologist Daniel Goleman, "emotionally intelligent."

Living an inauthentic life denies us the possibility of ever feeling truly loved for who we are. Caught in a relentless quest that can never be satisfied, it's impossible to feel loved when we haven't exposed who we are to others, even those closest to us. When our partner tells us that they love us, a little voice in the back of our mind says, "You love who you think I am, but if you really knew who I am, you wouldn't love me."

It's only when we both reveal ourselves fully that the purest love can be exchanged. The remedy for engaging more fully is to first be in touch with what we are feeling and then to express rather than repress, connect rather than protect, and reveal rather than conceal.

Like the development of any new skill, it may take a while to learn to live more openheartedly. Old habits take a while to break. Even if we feel awkward and clumsy, we can practice patience and forgiveness with each other and with ourselves as we stumble towards enlightenment. It's not about doing it right; it's about what Buddhists refer to as making "right effort." As we become more skilled at emotional honesty, we come to know ourselves and each other more deeply. And that is the reward for making that effort.

46.

When intrapersonal conflicts become interpersonal

C onfused. Conflicted. Mixed feelings. These are terms used to describe a conflict between two perspectives. When a conflict shows up in a relationship, it's interpersonal. When it exists within one person, it is intrapersonal. When an inner conflict isn't adequately resolved, it often manifests itself as a relationship breakdown.

The recognition that the root of an unresolved interpersonal issue may be an intrapersonal conflict can diminish or even prevent relational distress. Many arguments continue because each partner is dealing with a proxy rather than facing the person with whom the real difference of opinion lies: themselves.

Consider the example of Kit and Jessica. They dated in high school and married when they were twenty-one and nineteen, respectively. When they were each in their mid-thirties, Kit decided to go to college. Jessica decided to go also. They enrolled in a local state college and things went fine, until they reached the end of the first semester. That's when tensions between them started to build.

Kit is a pretty laid-back guy whose way of dealing with stress is to relax and give himself time to cool down when his mind gets overheated. Jessica, on the other hand, gets anxious when there are loose ends between them, so she prefers to address concerns as soon as she becomes aware of them. Her preferred style is to jump into things as quickly as possible. That helps to alleviate the anxiety she feels when there are incompletions on the back burner. You can probably see where this is going.

When they went back to school, Jessica made an effort to coerce Kit to study with her on a fixed schedule so that they could support each other. Kit, being Kit, didn't go for that idea, which seemed too inflexible. He preferred to have the option of studying when it worked best for him. Not surprisingly, their strategies ran headlong into each other with predictable results.

Kit: "It seemed like it really meant a lot to Jessica for us to create the same study schedule, so I begrudgingly agreed to give it a try. I made a real effort to accommodate Jessica's preference, but it just wasn't working for me. It wasn't that I wasn't trying hard enough; I was probably trying too hard. I suppressed my frustration in order to avoid an argument. That ended one day when I blew up at Jessica and yelled at her to 'Get off of my back!'"

In trying to placate her, Kit failed to take the downtime he needed to refill his tank. Jessica was afraid that Kit wouldn't have the self-discipline to study and that he would end up quitting college again, and so she "supported" him by reminding him of their study times and monitored his work. The more she oversaw Kit, the more resentful he became until the day of the blowup.

Jessica: "When Kit exploded at me, I was shocked but also curious as to why he was so upset. His anger seemed out of proportion to the situation. The good thing about the blowup was that it got our attention and made it clear to us both that something was going on that needed attention. At first, I was hurt and angry in response to Kit's outburst. We both got defensive, but things started to cool down a little after we took a break and came back together. Kit told me how frustrated he was and that he felt I had been nagging him and trying to control him. At first, I tried to explain why I felt the need to oversee him. That didn't help. What did help was when we both started talking about the concerns we had been withholding in an effort to keep the peace."

Kit: "Not only did we fail to keep the peace, but our unwillingness to express our feelings just made the situation worse. After we cleared the air, to my surprise, Jessica thanked me for being honest with her. This was the first time in my life that someone who had been upset with me actually thanked me for making them feel bad."

Jessica: "I really did feel grateful to Kit because it became clear to me how we had both been tiptoeing around trying not to upset each other and had ended up creating the exact outcome we wanted to avoid. We both have always wanted our relationship to be honest and trusting, but neither of us had seen how withholding our feelings was actually dishonest. It was a relief to find out that we could take each other's honesty without damaging or losing our relationship. That had been one of my fears."

Kit (to Jessica): "It felt awful when you checked up on me, trying to make sure that I was doing what you thought I was supposed to be doing. I got sick of always trying to please you! I never asked you to manage me."

Jessica: "Yes, I know you never asked me to take on that role. I'm not blaming you for my doing it. I admit that I take it on whenever I get scared that you're not going to handle things. I have high expectations of you and of myself."

Kit: "That's good to hear. Thanks for admitting that. Sometimes I feel like I'm the only one who disappoints you. I make an effort to accommodate you so that you won't get angry."

Jessica: "And you end up feeling frustrated because I can be hard to please."

Kit: "Bingo!"

Jessica: "Do you think it would help if I worked on backing off?"

Kit: "'Duh! Do you think it would help if I were more consistent in keeping my word?"

Jessica: "What a concept! Is that even possible?"

Kit: "I think we're onto something here. I would have to give up blaming you for pushing me. Tell you what: you push me less, and I'll push me more. I want you to trust that I really mean what I'm saying. I'm not promising to be perfect. I'm just saying that I feel more committed to my own integrity than I ever have before."

Jessica: "I believe you. And even though I don't feel certain that we've got this one licked yet, I do feel confident that we've made some real headway. I'm excited about what we have to look forward to."

Kit: "Me too."

They kiss.

This discourse between Kit and Jessica did occur, but it unfolded in a series of several counseling sessions. They finally recognized that they were each withholding their feelings not only from each other but from themselves as well. As they acknowledged their denied emotions, the tension between them diminished greatly.

When we come to terms with our commitment to protect rather than connect, we can defuse the tension in our relationship because that recognition often dissolves our ambivalence. When we find ourselves triggered, reacting out of proportion to our partner's perceived offense, there is a likelihood that something within us needs to be given attention. Doing so can mean the difference between defensive arguing and the productive communication that leads to peaceful coexistence.

47.

Are you checking in or checking out?

One thing successful couples do that struggling couples don't do enough of is checking in. This simple practice can mean the difference between relationship fulfillment and relationship hell. Checking in refers to the habit of taking a brief break from our daily responsibilities and redirecting attention to our inner experience. During a check-in, we focus on ourselves rather than external concerns. The purpose is to bring a nonjudging awareness to our thoughts, emotions, and physical sensations, and an unconditional acceptance of whatever we are experiencing.

This practice, also known as mindfulness, simultaneously quiets agitated thoughts, allowing us to relax into the present moment. Doing so enables us to see things as they are rather than through the filter of a distracted mind, and promotes a clearer perspective.

Checking in also refers to the process of becoming aware of the state of mind or mood of another person. We're expressing interest in their inner state. It can be through a simple question like "How are you?"—something people ask others sometimes several times a day. The difference, when we check in with that question is that we are really asking, not offering it simply as a greeting. In doing so, we're likely to get a different response than we would normally receive.

This interpersonal check-in is vital to all relationships since everyone's experience changes continually. If we are attuned to where others are in the present moment, we are more likely to be sensitive to their current state of being and able to (usually unconsciously) adjust the way in which we relate to them, creating a more mutually satisfying interaction.

We don't need to conduct this kind of an inquiry every time we start a new conversation. When we check in with each other, we are more able to orient to the other's current state of being. Charlie and I have both made a habit of checking in with each other first thing in the morning before we even get out of bed. It's been a great way for us to start the new day feeling aligned with each other. Even on those days when we're not exactly on the same page in regard to our prevailing moods, we have a sense of being connected and understood, which always makes for a good beginning to the day.

That feeling of connection strengthens the bond between two people and promotes feelings of mutual trust. Showing a sincere interest in another person's experience out of an intention to more fully understand them is also a way of showing respect and care for them. This can make the difference between merely spending time together and having emotional intimacy. Successful couples are not just exchanging household-related information; they are relating on a feeling level and speaking about things that truly matter to them.

Another form of checking in occurs through touch. Dr. William Masters, renowned sex researcher and sex therapist, is quoted as having told his trainees in the 1970s, "Tell your couples that twenty-four hours must not go by without some sensual touching." Without daily connections, we risk becoming roommates, business partners, or co-employees doing the job of parenting and home management. The spirit of love is often lost in the tasks inherent in creating a shared life. The juice of the relationship will inevitably dry up if it is not infused on a frequent basis with ample expressions of love. Even when physically separated, regular connection and check-ins—by phone, email, letter, text, Skype, or any other means of contact—will continue to enhance a relationship.

This simple act of connecting can prevent irritations from turning into major breakdowns. A little connection can go a long way!

48.

Putting an end to
"zero-sum thinking"

When there is a problem in a relationship, the first place most of us look is at the other person. This is an understandable response since it's easy to see where they may be to blame for the breakdown. While they almost certainly played a part in things having gotten to this point, this reflexive focus on the other person can result in an amplification of the problem rather than a diminishment of it. It is a convenient way to shift the spotlight of blame away from ourselves in a way that absolves us of responsibility. There's also a high likelihood that they are looking at us with the same lens of blame.

This process of mutual faultfinding rarely leads to a resolution. Casting blame on another is more likely to provoke defensiveness or hostility even when the accusation is true. Yet some kind of a response is called for, particularly if we are on the receiving end of another's accusations.

Most of us don't appreciate being told what's wrong with us, even if it's true. We might react with aggressiveness, out of a desire to defend our self-image and avoid vulnerability. This creates a problem for those of us who are concerned that if we don't do or say something to justify ourselves, the other person will get the idea that we agree with their position. They may take our lack of disagreement as an endorsement of their point of view. So where does this leave us?

It may seem that there are only two possibilities: suck it up or to get into a fight. At times, we can clear our feelings internally without having to bring them to the attention of our partner. This requires us to be honest with ourselves about whether we truly are able to let go of our feelings or whether we are simply avoiding the task of dealing with our partner directly. Some breakdowns, however, require immediate attention. Relationships can be challenging because they require us to be sensitive and responsive to the needs of the other person without neglecting our own needs. If we are too concerned about the other person, we risk being irresponsible to ourselves. If we are excessively preoccupied with ourselves, we risk neglecting our partner. If the other person feels like a loser, then we've both lost. The aftertaste of humiliation is likely to surface for the "loser" later on and diminish the trust level.

Rather than seeing the situation in terms of either standing up for ourselves or deferring to our partner, there is another possible outcome: recognizing the legitimate elements of each point of view. From this perspective we engage in dialogue that allows us to move from the position of opponents who wish to discredit the other person and their position to partners who share the same desire. We can create a mutually acceptable outcome.

Rather than focusing on what is wrong with the other person and trying to get them to admit their flaws, we can ask them questions that will provide us with the information that we need in order to support them in fulfilling their desires without abandoning our own. Doing so does more than provide us with information; it conveys to our partner a sense that we care enough about them to want them to get what they need. When we let go of accusatory judgments, the other person may become more conciliatory.

A "zero-sum" game is one in which only one partner can win. Arguments have unsatisfying outcomes when both partners approach them with zero-sum thinking. It's only when we stop seeing things in terms of winners and losers that satisfying outcomes are achieved. This allows potentially destructive arguments to be transformed from breakdowns into breakthroughs.

This requires the willingness to risk vulnerability and take the first step towards breaking the impasse rather than waiting for the other person to do so. Such vulnerability requires courage, intentionality, and responsibility. Like any other goal worth achieving, breaking the habit of zero-sum thinking doesn't happen overnight; it occurs over time and with practice. Fortunately, most relationships provide lots of opportunities to practice, and that's a good thing!

49.

Violence can come in many forms.

The dictionary defines violence as "injurious physical force, action, or treatment intended to inflict harm." The most important word in this definition is *intended*. What makes a behavior violent is the intention to inflict injury. This intention is not necessarily driven by a sadistic desire to create suffering. It may be motivated by the belief that a violent response is required in order to teach a lesson or to right a wrong. Ironically, when we default to violence, threatening conditions are inflamed, not diminished, and the likelihood of reprisal becomes greater.

Violence isn't limited to the use of physical force. It can be expressed in a variety of ways. Most of us are more tolerant of nonphysical forms of violence—such as intimidation, verbal threats, and menacing gestures—than of overt physical forms. Verbal violence involves the hurling of insults, threats, intimidating words, name-calling, and character assassination, all of which contribute to a weakening of the respect, and safety that are the bedrock of healthy relationships. Silence can be a form of violence when the intention is to punish or threaten. The violence of silence can be even more painful than verbal violence. The resulting feeling of disconnection can be especially painful to those who have experienced childhood trauma or abandonment. Many of us have been on both sides of the verbal violence equation and know what it feels like. Violence tears big holes in the fabric of trust. It can take days, weeks, months, or longer to grow back the trust that can be ripped apart in a moment.

The person acting violently is almost always driven by the fear that their needs won't be met. They use violence or threats of violence to gain control and fulfill their desires. Those who are prone to being violent can become suddenly triggered, often with no apparent cause. The challenge in dealing with a person who is threatening violence or being violent is to de-escalate tensions so that the fear or rage possessing them can begin to cool down, defusing their destructive impulses.

Just as making counterthreats is likely to amplify violence, tolerating violence out of fear also pours gasoline on the fire. It's natural to become defensive when accused of causing pain to another. Consequently, it's important to deliver feedback without critical judgment of the other person and focus on our response to their actions. For example, "When you shook your fist at me, I felt so frightened that I was unable to even hear what you said."

While seemingly less dangerous than physical violence, as we previously suggested, verbal violence can be as harmful as physical violence. The biggest casualty of verbal violence is the diminishment in the trust level of the relationship. When one partner is left feeling unsafe and fearful that a future eruption could occur at any time, they become careful about exposing their deeper feelings. Such fear makes the possibility of meaningful reconnection unlikely, if not impossible.

Depending on the seriousness of the violation caused by violence, restoration to a healthy degree of trust and mutual respect can take a long time and a lot of work. The potential consequences of using or tolerating violence are far greater than we may realize. Many of the people with whom we have worked that have experienced one or both sides of violence have told us that they did finally come to realize that the price of gaining control and domination was infinitely greater than they had realized. Some eventually did learn, but too late to heal the relationship and to avoid the pain of the loss and guilt they now live with on a daily basis. Some were more fortunate and salvaged their relationship before it was too late. But we never know when "too late" might come. Why take the chance?

50.

Beware of the dangers of arrogance.

We often write about the virtues and qualities that promote healthy and mutually fulfilling relationships, such as generosity, respect, commitment, and compassion, to name a few. Cultivating these qualities through intentional practice will do a lot to enhance the quality of all of our relationships. Strengthening virtuous qualities alone, however, is not sufficient to optimize the quality of relationships. We also need to identify those aspects of our character that not only do not support this intention but actually weaken it.

Of all the tendencies that can diminish the quality of our relationships, few, if any, are as damaging as arrogance. Arrogant as defined by the *American Heritage Dictionary* comes from *arrogate*, which means "to appropriate for oneself, presumptuously; to claim without right" and "to be overly convinced of one's own importance." Unfortunately, those who are guilty of possessing this trait often have no awareness of it. They can become combative when confronted with feedback that suggests they may be arrogant. Their invalidation of this feedback ironically provides evidence that such feedback is probably accurate.

Not surprisingly, when arrogance shows up in a relationship, it can be a conversation-stopper since the arrogant party is unlikely to loosen their grip on whatever they are committed to being right about. Arrogance is often an expression of a desire to prevent being ridiculed or punished by others by whom one feels threatened.

Consequently, efforts to influence others who are firmly attached to a position through reasonable, rational means are unlikely to be met with success. Trying to get such a person to be more open-minded is usually a losing battle. At best, there is a stalemate. At worst, things deteriorate and there is a serious degradation of trust and goodwill.

Resisting the temptation to argue with someone's point of view does not imply that you agree with them. When we respond to arrogance with a counter position, it almost always results in an inflammation of the antagonism between the two parties. Rather than trying to discredit another point of view or the person holding it, a more productive response is to acknowledge the other's perspective, even if it is spoken as a fact rather than an opinion.

A conversation can only deteriorate into an argument if both parties are trying to convert each other to their point of view. Stating, "I understand that that is your perspective, and I appreciate your sharing it with me" can be a good starting place. Adding the question "Are you interested in hearing about how I see it?" conveys our willingness to take no for an answer, which will lower the level of tension. More often than not, our partner will say yes. If they do, we have the opportunity to express our perspective without invalidating our partner's view. Doing so can promote trust, which will diminish the feelings of threat underlying the rigidity that characterizes arrogance.

The desire to "defeat" the arrogant person and strategies that accommodate disrespect are both doomed to fail. Although the vulnerability present in a nonreactive response to arrogance can enhance the likelihood of greater mutual understanding, this result is not always the outcome. If our partner says that they are not interested in hearing our point of view, we can respond by asking them to let us know under what conditions they might be. It's not about who is right but rather about being heard and understood. When these conditions are met, a mutual understanding can usually be worked out.

In dealing with arrogance, as with so many of the other "learning opportunities" relationships offer, Gandhi's advice to "be the change you want to see in the world"—or in this case, "in your relationship"—most definitely applies. The quality we most need to cultivate in order to influence another's arrogance is its opposite: humility. There is no guarantee that our partner will immediately thank us for enlightening them through our example and drop their defensiveness and open their heart to us. That may take another go-round or two, or more. But if we make our best effort and do what we know is the right thing, we'll have the comfort of knowing that we gave it our best shot, and at the very least, we didn't become part of the problem. Plus, who of us couldn't use a bit more humility in our lives? Regardless of the outcome, something positive will be gained. Humility is often contagious.

51.

Are you fighting or engaging in conscious combat?

Multiple-choice question: The factor most likely to predispose a couple to have an enduring successful relationship is . . .

A. Shared interests
B. Ability to prevent intense emotional conflict
C. Ability to manage differences effectively
D. Shared political views
E. Strong bonds of affection established early in the relationship

If you chose *C*, congratulations. You're one of a minority of people who recognize the necessity of having highly developed conflict management skills. All too many couples who start with strong feelings of affection can't imagine how such a need could ever arise. In the infatuation stage of relationship, the need to engage in responsible disagreements or "conscious combat" between two people who are so much in love seems inconceivable.

As veterans in the arena of relationships have come to learn, even relationships that begin in heaven can and often do expose shadowy parts of each partner. As these are gradually revealed, we are challenged to deal with our own and each other's less-than-ideal qualities with skill and compassion. As St. Francis puts it, the cultivation of the openheartedness that great relationships possess requires "a cup of understanding, a barrel of love, and an ocean of patience."

We need patience to accept the exposure of not only our partner's imperfections but also our own imperfect aspects. The belief that good couples don't or shouldn't fight can prevent us from admitting that we need to learn to manage differences skillfully. Since change involves stepping into the unknown, there will likely be some resistance to taking this step. The alternative is to ignore differences, which inevitably threatens the foundation of the relationship. Unaddressed differences erode feelings of affection, creating resentment, apathy, and bitterness.

The renowned marriage researcher John Gottman has studied thousands of couples in his Seattle "Love Lab" and identified these categories of relationships: validating, volatile and avoidant. The third group, the avoiders, are most at risk of having unsuccessful marriages. Their failure to address issues erodes what Gottman refers to as the couple's "fondness and affection system." While volatile couples may experience intense interchanges, addressing a difference directly, even unskillfully, is far better than avoiding them. Gottman found that the validating couples are the most successful. Yet even they have their share of differences that need to be addressed.

Successful couples generally don't come into their relationships with fully developed conflict management skills. Many bring a willingness to learn, openness towards each other's concerns, and a commitment to honesty. This intention is often born of appreciation for the intrinsic value of the relationship itself, creating a mutual sense of enlightened self-interest in which each partner is motivated by a desire to enhance the well-being of the other out of the recognition that they are enhancing their own happiness as well. As partners become less "me focused" and more "we focused," their need to control diminishes. Differences don't disappear; they simply become less significant. When these couples find themselves in conflict, their interactions, while passionate, are more likely to produce positive outcomes. This form of conflict management or conscious combat typically involves the following conditions:

- A willingness to acknowledge that a difference exists
- A stated intention on the part of both partners to work towards a mutually satisfying resolution
- A willingness to listen respectfully to each other's concerns, requests, and desires.
- A desire to understand what needs to happen in order for each person to experience satisfaction
- A commitment to speak without blame, focusing exclusively on one's own needs and concerns.

This process can be repeated until each partner feels that a satisfactory degree of understanding has occurred and there is a feeling of completion, at least for the time being. Completion does not imply that the matter is now settled once and for all but rather that an impasse has been broken or tension has been lowered sufficiently to allow for an appreciation of each partner's perspective. The expectation that differences should be completely resolved after a single interaction can set couples up for frustration that can intensify feelings of blame and shame. Committed partnerships provide lots of opportunities to engage in practices that strengthen the development of honesty, self-restraint, and generosity of spirit.

The idea of accepting this learning opportunity may (understandably) seem quite daunting, and it can be a formidable challenge. But it is well worth the effort, considering the value of the outcome of this process. The great philosopher Lao Tzu famously stated that "a journey of a thousand miles begins with a single step." What is a step you can take today to move that much closer to a fight-free zone in your relationship?

52.

Transforming your attachment into a preference

Kristen and Rob had been together for eleven years when he told her that he was quitting his well-paying job as a tech specialist for a billion-dollar company in Silicon Valley. "I've been feeling stifled and unappreciated for years, and I just got clear that I'm never going to feel fulfilled and creative as long as I'm under this company's or any other company's control as an employee. I know that my artwork is good enough to provide us with a decent income. It's just going to take a little time for me to establish myself as an independent agent." Rob wasn't asking for Kristen's permission to leave his job. Essentially, his message was "I've been thinking about making this move for a while, and I'm now clear that the time has come."

Although Kristen knew that Rob had been feeling unfulfilled in his job for a long time, she took it hard that they would soon have only her income to live on, until Rob's career as an artist was more firmly established. After listening to Rob's explanation about how he felt and why it was important to him to make the move now, Kristen reluctantly agreed to support his decision. But her anxiety about a diminishment in their income continued to grow. She turned to her friend Allison to get some perspective on her new circumstances.

Allison listened to her concerns and then pointed out that Kristen was assuming she knew what the future held for them— and that she was more concerned about the state of their financial affairs than she was the relationship. "Not that the finances aren't important; of course they are," Allison said. "You don't know for sure exactly how things are going to go in regard to future income. You may be right, but at this point your worrying is based upon nothing but speculation, and the truth is, you really don't know.

Allison continued, "I'm a recovering worrier too, and I often take great comfort in remembering what Mark Twain said about worrying: 'Worrying is like paying a debt you don't owe.' I've spent most of my life worrying about things that have never happened."

"I knew that Allison would be able to help me, and she did," Kristen told us, "with not only my worrying about finances but also my need to reprioritize our relationship to the top of the list."

Kristen took Allison's words to heart and pushed the pause button whenever she felt anxious by reminding herself that her assumptions were not necessarily true. Simply reflecting on the actual reality of the situation rather than the imaginings of her inflamed mind proved to be the most effective tool in her toolbox.

Kristen and Rob's income did take a drop in the months immediately following his resignation. Kristen had ample opportunity to work with her attachment to material comfort. She probed to see if Rob was open to working temporarily for his former employer, but he always refused. She could see how firmly positioned he was. She took more responsibility for creating more cash flow in her career. In realizing her relationship was at the top of her priority list, Kristen turned her attachment to material well-being into a preference.

When we last spoke to Kristen, she told us that she was very proud of the growing recognition Rob was receiving from their local art community, and for the stand he took for his own integrity. She also takes pride in how she learned to prevent the angry outbursts that in the past had diminished their trust. Her promotion at work and Rob's growing income from sales of his art eased Kristen's fears about becoming destitute.

"That fear," she said, "hardly ever comes up for me anymore. By learning to manage my reactive impulses and pause before I speak rather than blurt out my opinions, I've learned to bring an attitude of curiosity to other challenges besides our big career changes. Another big bonus I am enjoying is that I would not have been as motivated to develop my own career if Rob had stayed in computers with that abundant cash flow, and for that I am grateful."

What initially seemed to Kristen like an inevitable loss of security that would jeopardize their quality of life turned out to be a new chapter in their relationship. Her willingness to release her white-knuckle grip on the continuation of the status quo allowed for a new possibility to emerge. Sometimes what initially seems to be a distressing turn of events can be a blessing. You never know.

53.

To disclose or not to disclose

F ree-flowing communication is key to all successful relationships. Yet many of us choose to withhold what we fear will negatively influence our partner's impression of us. While reluctance to expose certain aspects of ourselves is understandable, there are inevitable consequences to withholding what is relevant to the relationship. Such concealment inhibits intimacy. While even those who value a high level of personal disclosure have a right to privacy, there is an important distinction between privacy and secrecy.

The difference has to do with intent. Keeping something to ourselves as a means of promoting a false impression is a form of dishonesty since the intention is to deliberately mislead the other person into believing something that isn't true. Not every detail of our past needs to be shared with a life partner, particularly that which has no relevance to our current relationship. Because many of us have had negative experiences revealing our feelings, we may have decided to be extra careful about what we reveal and to whom. If we were punished for telling the truth about what we did, said, thought, or felt, we may have learned to censor our responses to avoid the risk of activating others' disapproval.

While this sensitivity is understandable, there are inevitable consequences when our default response is to conceal rather than reveal, including a diminishment in spontaneity and authenticity. Partnerships characterized by a high degree of personal disclosure are vibrant because they are committed to sharing themselves authentically.

Breaking the habit of image management isn't easy, but it's definitely doable. When we have support from others who share that commitment with us, our progress is accelerated. And when one of those supporters is our life partner, there's no stopping us.

54.

Sometimes it's better to say nothing.

"Remember not only to say the right thing in the right place,
but far more difficult still, to leave unsaid the wrong thing at the
tempting moment."

—Benjamin Franklin

It is common to think of communication as being about what we say and how we say it. Yet sometimes, communication is enhanced not by what we say but by what we don't say. We may feel compelled to offer our opinion during a conversation, but doing so may not always be met with appreciation from the other person. While we may assume that they want or need advice from us, particularly if they are feeling distressed, that may not be what they are looking for.

Resisting the impulse to share our opinion doesn't mean that we say nothing in response to their expression of distress but rather that we listen carefully to their words and the feelings that underlie them. This may reveal what they hope to receive from us. If we're not clear as to exactly what that is, it's always a good idea to ask. A response a simple as "I'm sorry that you're having a hard time. I can understand why you're feeling upset. Is there anything that you need from me that might be helpful to you right now?"

This is not a script we are asking you to repeat but an example of a response that provides two things that often help provide support when our partner is in distress. The first part communicates our recognition of their situation, compassionate concern for them, and reassurance that they are not alone. The second part invites them to self-reflect to try to identify and communicate the desire they have at this time.

Their expression of distress is often motivated by a desire for help or the wish to fulfill an unmet need. Knowing what will be most helpful does not guarantee that we will be able to provide it, but in most cases, it will get us on the track of a productive interchange.

The root of the word *communication* is "common," which has to do with the creation of a common understanding and a shared concern for each other's well-being. Sometimes a moment of shared, caring silence can express more than a thousand words of advice. At other times, words may be called for. Words can heal and they can wound. What we say, whether or not we say anything, and how we say it can make all the difference in the world. It's helpful not only to seek to understand our partner's need in this moment but also to understand our own intention in responding to our partner, with the question "What is it that I really want to have happen through this interaction?"—simple words that can produce powerful results.

55.

Competing commitments

One of the messages we most frequently hear from our students and clients is "I know what I need to do, but I can't do it." Many of these folks have read a lot of self-help books, done workshops, and even gotten counseling, but despite their best efforts, don't seem to be able to implement the guidance they've received. They often conclude that their motivation to grow is weak, or that they're lazy or unintelligent—or just too screwed up to do what they think they should be doing. Yet what we often discover in speaking to them is that none of their assumptions about their deficiencies are true. In these cases, the answer to the question is two words: *competing commitments*.

A competing commitment is a (usually unconscious) commitment to something that competes with one's conscious desire. One example is the intention to have lots of free time and make a lot of money.

Another example is to choose between authenticity, which can feel risky, or to play it safe and minimize emotional disclosure. To enhance our relationships, we need to bring more transparency, truthfulness, acceptance, and awareness into our life. Which of these commitments are we choosing to honor?

This requires a commitment to integrity, honesty, and courage that overrides the ego's commitment to looking good, feeling good, and being right—in other words, willingness to honor our experiential truth rather than our ego's desires. The process requires an inquiry into ourselves that poses some powerful questions:

- What do I think I might see if I look more deeply within myself?
- If I don't like what I see, will I react to myself with compassion or with self-recrimination?
- Is there anyone in my life who might disapprove of something that I fear might be in me?
- What if there is a gap between who I think I am and how I actually live my life?
- What if I discover that I'm not the person I "should" be? Then what?

These are a few of the concerns that we might have when it comes to the commitment to avoid looking at ourselves and consequently any other concern that may threaten the identity we have created for ourselves. When we lift the prohibition on our "shadow commitment" of keeping unwanted insights out of our awareness, we become more able to recognize other hidden concerns.

Some other examples: I may have a conscious desire to become a better listener and an unconscious competing commitment to be the center of attention and gain approval by impressing others with my humor or brilliance. Or I may have a conscious commitment to being honest but an unconscious commitment to not reveal anything about myself that might cause others to think less of me. Or I might have a commitment to take better care of my body and also a belief that I deserve to indulge myself by taking a break from gym workouts or having a second helping of dessert. Or I might have a conscious desire to confront issues in my relationship honestly, but a hidden fear of conflict influences me to pretend that I'm not upset when I am. And the list goes on.

Bringing competing commitments into conscious awareness doesn't automatically make them go away, but it does enable us to recognize other desires we need to consider. It enables us to be less self-judgmental and to more deeply examine both sets of seemingly conflicting needs and to address the underlying concerns that require our attention. Expanding our capacity for self-reflection is one of the most important abilities that we can cultivate, not only in our relationships with others but also within the context of our relationship with ourselves. Doing so promotes self-understanding and self-acceptance, which enable us to bring greater acceptance and respect into all of our relationships.

56.

Boundaries: where do you draw the line?

A boundary is a line that marks a separation between two adjacent areas. Although we usually think of boundaries in geographical terms—for example, where one person's property ends and another's begins—this chapter refers to the line not between physical locations but rather in the emotional space between people.

Unlike physical boundaries like walls, personal boundaries are not immovable or even visible. Boundaries are the means through which we regulate the personal space between ourselves and others. They enable us to strike an optimal balance between physical and emotional closeness and distance. There is no fixed distance to which we can set our boundaries since the balance that fits our need depends upon many factors, including the circumstances in which we find ourselves, the person with whom we are relating, the level of trust we share with that person, and the present level of our need for connection.

The ability to set effective boundaries is an essential skill for all healthy relationships, and the failure to do so is a major contributor to many relationship breakdowns. Boundaries that are excessively rigid run the risk of keeping others at too much of a distance, diminishing intimacy, and creating an impression of detachment. Boundaries that are insufficiently clear create overaccommodation and excessive involvement in the lives of others.

Admittedly, setting effective boundaries is no easy task,

particularly if patterns of disrespectful reactions have been tolerated for years. Taking a stand for respect by communicating what is and is not acceptable puts us at risk of meeting some strong blowback from our partner. Sometimes things have to get pretty awful before we're finally ready to take the risk of taking a stand.

Skillful boundary setting conveys a clear message to others in regard to our level of physical and emotional comfort, which enables others to adjust their expectations accordingly. It also gives them permission to do the same in response to us. For many of us, however, doing so can be difficult because it requires us to break some old habits that we may have been reinforcing for years or even decades.

Habits such as saying "yes" when we actually feel "no" can feel risky since it brings up the fear of being rejected or disappointing others. But like many other risks, the benefits of breaking free from outmoded patterns greatly outweighs the consequences we fear may occur if we move from passivity and resignation to a stance of responsible boundary setting.

Linda: I know this to be true from my own experience. Years ago, during the early stages of our marriage, before I knew much about boundary setting, Charlie and I had gotten into some unhealthy patterns in which, out of my desire to avoid conflict, I became overly accommodating to Charlie to the degree that I had become toxic with resentment towards him. He became inflated with arrogance from getting his way whenever there was a difference between us. Although Charlie pushed back at the very beginning, when he saw that I meant business and that the new me was a lot more fun to be around, he came around, and we stayed together.

Here are some examples of the patterns that we were caught in and how I dealt with them: When Charlie didn't hold up his end of our responsibilities, rather than covering for him and doing it myself, and steaming in silent rage, I stopped rescuing him from his responsibilities. Surprise, surprise, he started to do more. Rather that criticizing him for being distant, I told him that I missed him and got vulnerable rather than angry. When I felt that he was taking advantage of my generosity without reciprocating, I told him that I was disappointed rather than calling him selfish. When I felt that he was relegating me to an inferior role in the family, it opened up a conversation about equality.

I saw that I had created the monster by feeding it with compliance and indulging Charlie's sense of entitlement. Instead of being manipulative, I began to express my desires directly. It was hard for me to accept my own culpability in our situation because it meant letting go of my victim story. What I didn't see then was that in withholding my true needs and desires, my feelings of weakness and powerlessness intensified. In moving from a victim identity to a more proactive position, I gradually began feeling more confident and self-assured.

During this time of transition from a hierarchical power structure to a partnership model, there were times when we slipped into our old patterns, but we were able to switch back with increasing swiftness. My fear diminished, as did our reactivity to each other, and we came to reach a higher level of mutual trust than what we had previously experienced. Learning to establish and honor effective boundaries was a major factor in that process!

57.
Manipulation: The costs outweigh the benefits

T he dictionary defines *manipulate* as "to influence or manage shrewdly or deviously or falsify for personal gain." No one likes to see themselves as, or be accused of, being a manipulator. But most of us from time to time engage in manipulative strategies in an effort to fulfill our expectations. We've come up with about fifty forms of manipulation. We consider these the top ten:

- Intimidation
- Shaming
- Threatening
- Insulting
- Ridiculing
- Accommodating
- Criticizing
- Flattery
- Bribing
- Guilt-tripping

Many manipulative behaviors are not intrinsically harmful and are under certain circumstances even appropriate. What determines whether or not one is being manipulative is not the behavior itself but the context in which it is being used and the intention behind the action or words. An intention is manipulative when it is driven by an unstated, covert desire that is meant to mislead.

Many of us are aware that manipulation in close relationships can diminish trust. Why then would we manipulate when we know better? And how do we justify this behavior to ourselves? Here are a few examples of some of the more commonly used rationalizations we've heard from people over the years:

- Everybody does it.
- It's harmless.
- I won't get my needs met if I don't.
- He/she does it, and I'll be at a disadvantage if I don't.
- It's not a big deal.
- It's a habit and I can't give it up.
- I don't want anyone to take advantage of me.

You can add your own favorites to this list. Keep in mind that rationalizations aren't equivalent to the truth. In the case of relationships, unintended consequences inevitably occur when we justify manipulations.

Those consequences include:

- A diminishment in the level of trust in the relationship
- An increase in feelings of anxiety resulting from the fear of one's deeper motives being revealed
- Feelings of guilt and shame
- A diminishment in the quality of intimacy
- An increase in feelings of resentment
- An increase in the frequency and intensity of arguments
- A loss of personal integrity

While we may feel manipulated when another person is using covert means to influence us, we are much less likely to be aware of these intentions in ourselves. It is embarrassing to catch ourselves in the act. Most of us are disinclined to recognize motivations that are inconsistent with our self-image as being a good person. Consequently, we are generally unaware of our manipulative tendencies.

We usually manipulate because we fear that if we don't fulfill our desires, we will suffer. Examples of the desires we might seek to fulfill include (but are not limited to) acceptance, love, approval, sex, money, attention, security, support, agreement, control, and praise. In becoming more conscious of our manipulative patterns and the cost incurred, we can find the motivation to interrupt these impulses. Then we can find the courage to risk outwardly acknowledging our needs and desires by making direct requests.

The process of interrupting manipulation to restore integrity requires us to get honest with ourselves. Through a process of self-inquiry, we can bring into greater awareness the unconscious motivators at play. Self-inquiry enables us to use more effective means to meet our needs.

Here are some questions that can help uncover some of our unrecognized motivations. Respond to these questions in writing or in dialogue with another person rather than simply think about the answers. With each insight into our deeper motivation, we become more empowered to act in ways that strengthen our integrity.

- What are your preferred forms of manipulation? (Examples of ways that you manipulate)
- What are you looking for when you manipulate? (Examples of what you are seeking to get or experience)
- What is the fear that drives you to manipulate? (Another way to ask this question is "What are you afraid of losing or not getting if you don't manipulate?")
- What are the prices you pay for manipulating? (What are the negative consequences to you and your relationships?)
- What would be required of you to stop manipulating? (What risks would you have to be willing to take in order to break this habit?)
- What kind of support will be useful to you in your efforts to break the habit of manipulation?
- What do you stand to gain by breaking the manipulation habit?

Such self-confrontation requires courage and commitment. The tendency to avoid facing unpleasant truths about ourselves is strong in us all, because examination can activate feelings of shame and guilt. Yet in coming to terms with these deeper feelings, we experience greater authenticity, intimacy, and passion in our relationship. These positive feelings begin to emerge as soon as we commit to communicating more directly with those with whom we seek to co-create fulfilling connections. The longer we practice, the easier it gets. It's never too early or too late to begin to enjoy the results!

58.
Mind over matter

The term *mindfulness* has been showing up a lot in the media lately. When people think of mindfulness, they often envision someone sitting on a zafu (meditation cushion) in a lotus position with eyes closed and a blissful expression on their face. While many people do practice mindfulness on meditation cushions, mindfulness can be experienced anywhere and anytime. Mindfulness refers to the process of bringing one's attention to inner experiences that include thoughts, emotions, and physical sensations. It has to do with directing awareness to our present-moment experience that is free of judgment.

While to the uninitiated the idea of observing our inner experience may seem simple, as anyone who has ever practiced this knows, simple isn't necessarily easy. Part of the challenge of being mindful is that our mind (and everyone else's) has a tendency to bounce from one object of attention to another, often within milliseconds. This phenomenon is often referred to as "monkey mind."

Living in a culture that subjects us to a continuous flow of distractions, the tendency for attention to be splintered is strong. When this happens, we can feel fragmented, like something is missing, and it is—a sense of wholeness. Because we're not fully present, we never feel quite complete, so we look for something or someone to provide us with what we need in order to feel whole.

A feeling of wholeness involves a sense of being at peace and being connected to ourselves and others. When we don't experience this, we might conclude that it is because we don't have enough of something, and therefore we seek to acquire it. The practice of mindfulness is not necessarily blissful. Since being mindful is about being present with our experience, whatever that may be at any given moment, the range of possibilities is vast. Being complete isn't necessarily synonymous with feeling good; it's simply about showing up and being with whatever is present in our awareness.

So, what does all this have to do with relationships? In a nutshell, everything. One of the primary motivations in seeking partners, temporary or permanent, is to find this sense of wholeness. The positive sensations that relationships provide are a powerful distraction from unpleasant feelings and fulfill our fundamental human need for connection. Practicing mindfulness can also neutralize reactive patterns that diminish trust and intimacy. Mindfulness in romantic partnerships can be a powerful form of daily practice. When couples share this sense of mutual presence, they are more open to the full range of their experience. This capacity for meaningful engagement is the foundation of fulfillment in relationships.

When we are more able to tame our wild mind by bringing a nonjudging awareness to our experience, we naturally become less reactive and more present, which diminishes the possibility of getting possessed by disturbing thoughts that are often the source of conflict.

Mindfulness in relationships can be practiced in a wide variety of settings: sitting quietly or taking walks together; speaking only that which is true and useful rather than indulging in judgments and unsolicited advice; designating uninterrupted time to get caught up on essential rather than practical concerns; deliberately choosing to share a meal slowly rather than rushing through it without savoring the food; or simply sitting together quietly. These activities can be done alone, with a partner, or in a group.

Mindfulness can be practiced in everyday life simply by slowing down and paying attention. Interrupting mind chatter with a reminder to check in and take a couple of conscious breaths provides relief from disturbing thoughts. Mindfulness is not an escape from responsibilities that require actions but a process that enables us to see more clearly in our relationships, in work, and in life in general.

And for those who would like to practice mindfulness but feel that they don't have enough time available to do it, consider this: His Holiness the Dalai Lama spends four hours a day sitting in meditation. And he doesn't exactly have an empty schedule. When something is important enough, we somehow manage to find time for it.

Living mindfully doesn't require us to sit in meditation or add anything to our already full life. It's just a matter of practicing presence with what we are already doing. Paradoxically, it doesn't mean getting less done, but just the opposite. Try it and see for yourself. You might like it.

59.

Family rules and family roles

The roles we played in our childhood family are often replayed in our relationships. We naturally seek partners with whom we can replicate these patterns. We adopted these roles as children in order to master the challenges of growing up in our original family. Here are some examples of these roles:

- The peacemaker's job it is to smooth over disruption in the family by being a mediator, in order to pacify those who are irritable and angry.
- The parental child is a premature adult. Parental kids are drafted not only into the practical parts of running a household, but also assigned exclusive responsibility for parenting younger siblings and/or under-functioning parents.
- The marital child fills the vacancy left by the literally or emotionally absent parent. They become a surrogate spouse whose job it is to fill needs for companionship and in extreme cases, even their parent's sexual needs.
- The helper acts as an assistant to the parent who may be physically or emotionally overwhelmed. As a result of the helping they do, they miss out on the pleasure of childhood play.
- The clown or comedian attempts to cheer up his depressed parent or parents.
- The hero makes good grades, excels at sports, gets elected to

student council, and in obvious ways is a credit to the family, but often feels lonely, insecure, and pressured.

- The rebel is a rule breaker. She won't clean up her room, won't do her homework, may skip school, get pregnant, drive too fast, or yell at adults, and is sometimes called the black sheep. This is the child willing to sacrifice herself in order to take the heat off the parents' troubled marriage.

These are a few of the many roles that we can be assigned in childhood. Consider the situation of Victor and Georgia, who had no awareness of the patterns they had dragged into their marriage from their childhoods and the destructive influence of those persisting roles.

Victor was a parental child. His father was an alcoholic who was frequently out of work, fired from jobs because of absences due to his being hungover. Victor saw his mother's distress and not only took after-school jobs to bring in money for the family but also became a strong emotional support to his mom. Victor's wife, Georgia, was the youngest in her family, and because her parents had such an empty relationship with each other, she became the object of their affection. They babied her and did not encourage her independence because of their own needs to hold on to her. She had very little time of her own to establish a sense of self between leaving her family and going straight to marriage. Due to her family's excessive helpfulness, Georgia thought of herself as helpless, needy, and weak.

In their early years together, Victor liked being seen as a superman and got used to having things his way. Georgia enjoyed being taken care of and pampered. But over time, his delight eroded, giving way to feeling burdened. The sexual attraction faded because he felt he was more of a father to Georgia than a husband. Victor's attempts to talk about the dilemma and change the pattern were ineffective.

The unconscious continuation of the over-functioning husband and the under-functioning, childlike wife took their family down, and eventually they divorced. If they had participated in therapy that addressed the old family roles running them, these two would have had a better chance of salvaging their marriage. The over-functioning husband with the under-functioning wife is but one of many patterns imported from original families that can exert a destructive force in adult relationships.

There are many others, all of them exhibiting the powerful corrosive force old patterns can have until they are brought out in the open to be deconstructed. The huge advantage of bringing the roles we played as a child up to conscious mind is that we then can see more clearly that as an adult, we have maturity, power, and, most importantly, the ability to make wiser choices. And that can make all the difference in the world!

60.

The biggest relationship threat

The esteemed relationship expert John Gottman uses the term *four horsemen of the apocalypse* to refer to four of the biggest threats to relationships: criticism, defensiveness, stonewalling, and contempt. According to the *American Heritage Dictionary of the English Language*, the definition of contempt is "reproachful distain, as for something vile or dishonorable, bitter scorn."

Contempt rarely comes "out of the blue," although it may seem that way to the person experiencing it or to the recipient of it. More often than not, it occurs as a result of denied disappointment, resentment or hurt. These feeling may have been accumulating over time, and our failure to address them has resulted in contempt.

Painful emotions don't necessarily disappear. In fact, they intensify until they are given adequate attention. Telling our partner that they have caused us pain can feel risky. We are opening the possibility that they may become upset with us, the bearer of news they'd rather not hear. For this reason, many of us withhold "bad news," hoping the feelings will go away and we won't have to say anything. Often this is not the case. The problem is that when we fail to resolve a difference, negative feelings don't just remain; they can erode the foundation of the relationship. This is like going from being unhappy to being depressed. The higher level of disturbance (depression or contempt) is much more difficult to recover from due to the strength of the grip it has on us. The longer the issues remain unaddressed, the more likely they will create a polarizing impasse in which neither partner sees any viable option other than leaving or enduring continued suffering. Trying to tolerate a situation characterized by contempt is damaging not only to the relationship but also to each partner's emotional and physical well-being.

Contempt often results from an unwillingness to initiate difficult conversations. When both partners can respond to feedback without becoming defensive, contempt is unlikely to occur because there will be no fear—or at least little fear—of retaliation for bringing up the tough issues.

The tendency towards contempt is a habit created by both partners. Often one partner is conflict avoidant and the other is not; the avoider is inclined to nurse grudges and destructive fantasies. Over time, if unchecked, these feelings can destroy even good relationships. The key word here is *unchecked*. When we check in to our relationship and respond in a respectful manner, we're much less likely to slide into contempt. When we check out of our relationship, we are sowing the seeds of contempt and putting our own well-being and the relationship at risk.

It can take courage and commitment to respectfully raise issues with our partner that involve the possibility of conflict. While there is a risk in opening up potentially inflammatory subjects, that risk is greatly outweighed by the consequences of refusing to address differences that need resolution. Although we can't prevent feelings of anger or disappointment from arising, we can prevent them from degrading into contempt. And that's a good thing!

61.

Triggered? Try this.

I t's easy to fall into the trap of polarized thinking—the kind of thinking that tells us things are one way or the other, "my way or the highway," right or wrong, good or bad. When it comes to relationships, this kind of thinking is likely to get us into trouble. So, what do we do when we find ourselves in a position in which we are emotionally triggered and either/or thinking takes over? It looks like we've only got two options: to either discharge feelings we have towards the person who has triggered us or to stuff our emotions. But here's the good news; there is a third option available, and that is something called "pause and reflect."

Pausing has to do with the process of redirecting our attention away from our partner (who we might see as an adversary) and towards our inner dialogue. At this point it becomes possible to shift our intention from being right to creating a respectful dialogue, rather than perpetuating a win-lose scenario. When one player wins at the cost of the other person feeling like a loser, the "victory" comes at too great a cost to be worthwhile. Indulging in the desire to defeat or punish our opponent will likely diminish mutual trust and goodwill.

It only takes one person to initiate a shift from an adversarial to a partnership perspective. The challenge is to be willing to take this step rather than try to coerce the other person to do it first. This change in perspective immediately promotes a feeling of greater safety for both partners, and makes it easier to listen and respond to each other less defensively.

Here are some of the things to remember when our "hot buttons" are activated:

- My partner hasn't made me feel this way (hurt, angry, scared, etc.), but they have activated these feelings in me.
- It's okay to feel my feelings, but I don't necessarily have to punish or blame my partner for activating them.
- I want them to know that I don't see things the way they do and that I have a right to my point of view. The best way to do this is to lower their level of defensiveness by not threatening or condemning them and expressing my concerns.
- I know that it feels good to counterpunch when I feel that I have been unfairly treated, but doing so will only dig us both deeper into a hole.
- I also don't want to accept the blame for this breakdown when I don't feel that I deserve to assume all of it.
- I know that I need to accept my responsibility without giving up myself or making it my partner's fault.

We need positive self-talk to be able to ask and answer ourselves when we're in the heat of an emotional interaction. And yes, this is easier said than done. It's helpful to remember that during highly stressful interactions, we can always take a brief break. On the break, we clear any punitive and defensive impulses we have. Triggering occurs even in great relationships, but partners can neutralize triggers quickly because they recognize them sooner. In doing so, the triggers become a blip on the screen rather than a major breakdown. And this is something we can all learn to do.

62.

Irreconcilable differences

E ven the most successful partnerships contain differences that cannot be resolved completely. Some differences are deal-breakers if one or both partners can't tolerate them. But when there is a foundation of love and respect, a breakup is less likely to occur.

Many of the differences couples have in the early stages of their relationship never disappear but don't become problematic. It's only when they become a source of conflict that problems arise. When we can accept and even appreciate differences as an inevitable aspect of any relationship, we will likely no longer view them as a threat. If our differences aren't a threat, we'll become less attached to our personal preferences, making even the most irreconcilable of differences more manageable.

Consider the case of Leah and Jason, whose marriage had deteriorated into a destructive downward spiral that threatened to land them in divorce court.

Leah: "Before Jason and I got married, I thought that couples became more harmonious over time and their differences diminished or disappeared. Boy, was I wrong! Not only did our different points of view not go away, but they actually became more pronounced and inflamed. I was terrified that if this continued, our marriage would be doomed."

Jason: "Things looked pretty hopeless for a while. I've always had a thing about being controlled, and I went crazy every time Leah tried to get me to do something I didn't feel right about."

Leah: "And that just triggered my fear that Jason didn't love me. I thought that if he did, he would be more open to my input."

Jason: "We kept getting locked into these horrible patterns that were squeezing the life out of our marriage. To say that it was a nightmare would be an understatement."

Leah: "By the time we finally got help, we were on the brink of divorce. One of the issues that we couldn't agree on was that I wanted us to get counseling and Jason didn't."

Jason: "I've always believed that if you put your mind to something, and worked hard to straighten out your problems, you should be able to handle things on your own. Fortunately, Leah took a stand and wouldn't back down on this, and I begrudgingly agreed to go."

Leah: "We literally had nothing to lose. Our relationship was completely trashed, we were living like enemies, we hadn't had sex in months, and things were getting worse by the day."

Jason: "The counselor helped me to see some of the ways I was getting in my own way. He pointed out some of my negative behaviors, and alternatives to them."

Leah: "Jason's a very good student. If there's something he wants to learn, he throws himself into it; that's the way he engaged in the counseling process."

Jason: "The counselor helped me to see that underneath my anger was a lot of fear that Leah might see me as weak if I didn't stand up to her. Until we got counseling, I didn't think that I was part of the problem. Eventually, I came to realize that Leah wasn't the only one who was being stubborn."

Leah: "I had to learn to manage my fears of losing Jason, the ones that caused me to try to control him. One of the most important things I learned was that our differences weren't the problem; it was our efforts to convert each other to our own perspective. As we began to see that the differences didn't have to go away, we both relaxed our campaign to get the other person on our page. These days, we each just communicate our preferences without the need to get the other person to agree. We usually come to a workable understanding because we never try to coerce each other into anything . . . well, hardly ever."

Jason: "It's taken a lot of practice. Our counselor got us started, but then it was up to us to implement the things we learned from him. Changing old habits isn't easy; we had plenty of learning opportunities. In the process, we've each become more appreciative of our differences, and more committed to accepting influence from each other."

Leah: "I've developed more patience and forgiveness. For a couple of recovering hotheads, we live a remarkably harmonious and peaceful life now."

Leah and Jason salvaged a marriage that was on life support by being willing to make their relationship more important than playing out lifelong patterns of control and manipulation. They put their relationship at the top of their priority list and risked it all to go for the real gold that is available in committed partnerships. There is an old saying: "You can be right, or you can have a relationship." The key word is *or*. We can't have it both ways. What's your choice?

63.

Don't use these three words.

"You're being defensive!" If you've ever been on the receiving end of these words, you know that the last thing you feel like doing upon hearing them is to let down your guard. Ironically, that's probably exactly what the person delivering this message is trying to get you to do. If you weren't defensive before you heard this accusation (and it is usually expressed as an accusation), you almost certainly will be after hearing it.

Defensiveness is a natural response to the perception of a physical or emotional threat. With practice, we can learn to replace unskillful forms of self-protection with those that are more effective. While many self-help books warn of the perils of getting defensive or provoking defensiveness in others, they often fail to acknowledge how difficult it can be to eliminate this instinctual response.

The impulse to defend ourselves when we feel attacked, particularly by someone with whom we have an intimate relationship, can be strong, sometimes overwhelming. It may seem out of proportion to the perceived offense because the words or behavior to which we are reacting may be activating unhealed emotional wounds. When our "hot buttons" are triggered, we are possessed by emotions that are usually kept beneath the surface of our conscious awareness.

There are consequences to keeping these feelings underground. They include many forms of distress that impact our health and the health of our relationships. Until we can come to terms with our past, they remain "incompletions" that we will likely feel compelled to avoid. Consequently, they continue to block the flow of our creative energy, inhibit our capacity for intimacy, and cause us to live with low-level anxiety resulting from a fear of exposing potentially volatile emotions.

It's not easy to simply let go of painful feelings or thoughts. Until we identify the fears and beliefs that drive our reactive patterns, we will continue to be enslaved by them. Committed partnerships provide ongoing access to those underlying concerns. They activate our deepest longings, greatest fears, and strongest desires, primarily because they often reawaken unhealed injuries. In addition, committed partnerships hold our most cherished hopes. These desires, however, often turn into expectations that aren't always known to our partner or even to ourselves.

Furthermore, in many cases, it's probably not possible for a single human being to meet them all. But that doesn't stop us from believing that they should. We may feel entitled to have our expectations fulfilled and become angry when our partner "betrays" us by failing to live up to what we believe we have a right to expect. No one else in our life holds the power that we project onto a life partner. When we feel disappointed by them, the pain can be excruciating, and when we feel fulfilled by them, our joy can be boundless.

One of the ways in which we attempt to avoid the pain of disappointment is by trying to control our partner's behavior. Defensiveness is one such example of control. Defensiveness can take a variety of forms, including intimidation, withdrawal, blaming, self-justification, interrupting, explaining, or counterattacking, to name a few. Ironically, engaging in controlling behaviors intensifies the conditions that initiated the conflict in the first place.

The solution to this impasse is not about changing our behavior as much as it is about shifting the perspective from which we view a given situation. As long as we see our interaction as a breakdown caused by the other person, we will feel the need to "correct" them. They, in turn, may counter our controlling efforts by amplifying their defensiveness. The cycle can, and often does, continue with predictably unpleasant results. It's possible to interrupt this pattern by shifting our perspective from that of a victim to that of a responsible agent who has the power to defuse a volatile situation by dropping defensive behavior.

The habit of defensiveness is not one that dissolves easily, even when we commit to neutralizing our emotional buttons. Knowing what we need to do is not always enough to do it. Our conflicting commitments, such as those to control, seek approval, protect ourselves, or be right, often override our willingness to be vulnerable and transparent.

Despite these conflicting desires, it *is* possible for any couple to interrupt the defensive patterns that show up in their relationship. Yes, it does take effort, practice, and courage to expose our vulnerable emotional underbelly in the face of fear. But regardless of the outcome, in the process we can become more loving and lovable, which greatly enhances the likelihood of creating the outcome that we each desire.

And about those three words: when you feel the impulse to use them, you might want to ask yourself, "What, if anything, might I be doing or saying that is causing my partner to feel defensive?" If you are unable to come up with something, they will surely be willing to answer your question. And at that point you've got a brand-new conversation available.

64.

Can I give you some feedback?

If this question makes you feel like running for the nearest exit, it's not surprising. When most of us hear the word *feedback*, we expect one or more of the following: judgments, advice, opinions, or constructive criticism. The unspoken assumption in offering this "help" is that we (the listener) don't really know what we should do or say, how we should do it, or even what's good for us. And that they—the speaker who is offering the gift of their feedback—does know.

The intention behind an offer to give feedback isn't necessarily based on a desire to serve another's best interest. It could also be coming from a wish to affirm one's intelligence by sharing wisdom, thereby demonstrating superior knowledge. This is not always the case. Advice is frequently given from a genuine intention to serve another's best interest, and that is fine; but that's not feedback.

Part of the problem lies in a widespread misunderstanding about the meaning of the word itself. Simply put, what most people call feedback isn't. In the context of relationships, feedback is information that describes one's response, usually resulting from an interaction with another. Feedback is not an assessment of another's behavior or words but is one's internal response to another. No one can know with certainty how others are impacted by interactions, and without feedback we can only speculate as to what someone is experiencing. Whether we realize it or not, we are constantly scanning others' responses, both verbal and nonverbal, in order to determine whether we need to modify our message or its delivery.

Cues that involve body language, such as raised eyebrows, quickened breathing rate, changes in posture, leaning forward (or back) in one's chair, smiles, or frowns, are all examples of feedback to which we unconsciously respond by modifying our words, tone of voice, or behavior. If we conclude that the person to whom we're speaking is bored, irritated, disengaged, impatient, or exhibiting any signs that tell us they may not be fully present or are resistant to what we are saying, we may choose to modify the content or tone of our delivery.

We can ask if they understand what we're saying or whether they agree with us in an effort to get more information, or request that they paraphrase our message in their own words. Feedback is distinct from judgments, interpretations, opinions, advice, beliefs, or suggestions. It is simply an expression of one's sensations, emotions, and thoughts that arise in response to being on the receiving end of a communication.

For example, if my friend asks me for feedback on an issue that concerns him, I wouldn't tell him what I think he should do. My response would reflect my internal response upon receiving his message. Examples of feedback could be "I felt pressured to agree with you" or "I am confused" or "I felt supported and understood by you" or "I'm not exactly sure what you're asking me." What isn't feedback: "I wouldn't do that" or "That's a good idea" or "Are you nuts?" or "I wouldn't let her get away with that" or anything that includes advice. It's not that opinions can't be valuable; they're just not feedback. If I'm uncertain of whether my friend wants an opinion or actual feedback, I might ask for clarification so that I can give the kind of response he is actually looking for.

When there is confusion, the likelihood of a misunderstanding increases. Sometimes when people request feedback, they're looking for agreement or approval. A receiver must have a certain level of skill to deliver feedback that is sensitive, accurate, and useful. Giving honest feedback exposes the giver to the possibility of saying something that could have an unpleasant impact on the receiver. The giver of feedback must be willing to risk an upset and trust that there is a mutual intent to work out any difficulties that may arise.

Feedback should only be given when it has been clearly established that the speaker really wants it. Unsolicited advice or judgment is likely to be unappreciated, regardless of how truthful or accurate it may be. When in doubt, check things out.

Since the underlying intention of much communication is to create a particular response in the listener, feedback is an invaluable instrument. If we don't have access to this information, we have no way of determining how successful we have been in our communication and what, if any, adjustments we need to make.

One of the greatest benefits of exchanging feedback is that it promotes greater understanding. Embedded in the request for feedback is the implication that the speaker trusts the listener and values their response. Thus, every time feedback is delivered, there is the potential for a deepening of trust.

Balancing self-awareness with honesty and sensitivity requires a high degree of skill, but with practice it is possible to master this art. The best coaches, lovers, managers, leaders, teachers, and parents have done that. Most didn't start at the top of their game; they got there by paying attention to the feedback that life naturally generates, noticing the consequences of their words and actions, then integrating the lessons into their lives. Simple, but not necessarily easy, and definitely worth a try.

65.

From fear to fearlessness

Of all the qualities and character strengths that are necessary for the creation of great relationships, courage is one we would put at the top of the list. The reason for this is simple: when courage is lacking, the will to live openheartedly cannot prevail.

Without courage, we cannot risk exposing the soft underbelly of our emotions to others. The word *fearlessness* is synonymous with the word *courage*, so we will use those words interchangeably in this chapter. According to the dictionary, courage is "the ability to do something that frightens one; strength in the face of pain or grief." There is nothing there about not having fear. In fact, it suggests that you can only be fearless or courageous if you have fear.

Here's what a few other people who know a thing or two about courage have to say about it:

"Courage isn't the absence of fear; it is the ability to act
in the face of fear"

—Bruce Lee

"Courage isn't the absence of fear, but the triumph over it."

—Nelson Mandela

"Fearlessness is not the absence of fear. It's the mastery of fear. It's about getting up one more time than we fall down."

—Arianna Huffington

"Each time we face our fear, we gain strength, confidence and courage in the doing."

—Theodore Roosevelt

"Courage isn't the absence of fear, it's the acting in spite of it."

—Mark Twain

The word *courage* has its origin in the French word *coeur*, from the Latin *cor*, both of which mean "heart." To be fearless, we must lead from the truth of our heart rather from the fear in our mind. This does not negate the validity of our concerns regarding the possible dangers that lie before us, but despite those, we make a conscious choice about our primary intention in this moment and what action best represents our heart's desire. It does not mean that we should react recklessly but that we carefully make our choice and proceed consciously rather than automatically, taking responsibility for our actions.

When we are wounded or feel threatened in a relationship, our feelings may get hurt. It takes courage to resist the temptation to become defensive and withdraw in the face of fear, and instead move forward. The late, great spiritual teacher Stephen Levine called this "keeping your heart open in hell." We can't help but experience fear when we feel threatened, but we can determine how we respond to it. Honoring our deeper intentions rather than indulging our impulses to withdraw or attack will strengthen our courage muscle.

Becoming fearless requires us to allow ourselves to experience aversion as well as desire, and to engage both sides. If desire is strong and the expected rewards are high, we can commit ourselves to going forward even in the face of fear. We don't necessarily begin with a brave heart; we develop it along the way. We begin from wherever we are right now by putting put one foot in front of the other; then repeat.

66.
Primum non nocere

rimum non nocere. You may be more familiar with this term when you see or hear it in a language other than Latin. The English translation is "First to do no harm." It is part of the Hippocratic oath, a vow that physicians take to uphold specific ethical standards in their practice of medicine. This admonition could easily apply to many other arenas as well, especially relationships. It seems pretty obvious that creating harm is something that anyone would want to avoid doing, particularly when it comes to relationships.

Few, if any of us, have never experienced a moment of frustration, anger, pain, or terror in which we feel an impulse to do or say something hurtful to someone whom only moments earlier we had felt warm and tender feelings for. Most of us are usually able to resist the temptation to lash out at someone who seems to have suddenly transformed into an evil demon before our very eyes. Yet we all have days in which our ability to exercise self-restraint fails miserably and we blurt out words that we regret. Everyone makes mistakes. But is it really a mistake when we actually want to hurt the person that we have just unloaded on? Not to say that it is necessarily our intent, but (let's get honest here) sometimes it is. Those shadowy impulses that reside within us can, and under certain circumstances will, get expressed when we're having a bad day, or when we're overtired, emotionally depleted, or feeling overwhelmed with stress that narrows our emotional bandwidth to a thin sliver.

Although there is no way to prevent meltdowns from occurring, we can minimize their frequency and intensity by remembering the oath physicians vow to live by. Committing to honor a vow of harmlessness will definitely make us less vulnerable to the darker forces lurking below the surface of our awareness until we experience a strong provocation. The closer we are to someone, the easier it is to be provoked, since there is a lot more at stake with our primary relationships than with people with whom our expectations are of a lower order. We often associate the concept of causing pain with physical harm, which certainly can be a form of injury. There are, however, many forms of harm other than physical that can be at least as painful as physically striking someone. As many of us know from our own experience, that old saying that "sticks and stones can break my bones, but words can never hurt me" is untrue.

Words can and do hurt us when they are used in a way that is punitive. We've worked with people who have experienced both physical and emotional abuse, and for many of them, the verbal abuse hurt more than the physical abuse because it was directed at a sore or unhealed spot in their heart. Most of us are more careful about restraining impulses to physically hurt others than we are impulses to emotionally hurt others. We tend to underestimate the depth of the injury words can cause because the evidence of the damage is less obvious. It behooves us all to remember the power, both negative and positive, of our words and to pause for a moment before we act on the impulse to let it rip!

67.
The hidden cost of people pleasing

"I f you don't have something nice to say, don't say anything at all."
          "Be nice to your sister."
"That's not nice."

What's the common word in these three statements?

You're right! *Nice* answer.

It's nice to be nice. But can you be too nice? In a word, yes. The danger in being excessively nice is that you run the risk of being inauthentic, and possibly dishonest. And that's not nice. The dictionary defines *nice* as "agreeable, pleasant, satisfactory, and good-natured." There's nothing wrong with that, except this one thing: If we've been brought up to hold "niceness" as a condition for others' approval, we might get the idea that we need to be nice at all times, with all people, and if we're not, we risk losing our relationship or being punished. And if we feel obliged to always fulfill this requirement, any part of us that we don't consider to be nice never gets to show up. Those parts include anger, power, intensity, ambition, and tenacity. When we demonize and deny aspects of ourselves, the result is that our sense of self-worth diminishes.

Needing to be nice and seeking approval are two sides of the same coin. Social creatures that we are, most of us favor acceptance over rejection, and prefer to be liked rather than disliked. Things become problematic when we need others' approval in order to feel okay. This occurs when we don't experience acceptance and self-approval and therefore try to figure out other ways to earn it. For example, we might excel in a certain activity or sport, get excellent grades in school, make people laugh, and make lots of money proving that we're smart and successful. If we believe that we can't do any of these things, we might think there's always the one thing we know we can do: be nice!

Please note that this is not a criticism of niceness or of people who are kind, considerate, and conciliatory. Those are commendable qualities, and the world could certainly use more of them. But there is a difference between choosing to be these things and needing them in order to feel worthwhile.

When we feel that we *need* to be nice, we are motivated by fear of the consequences of not fulfilling this mandate. We can feel trapped and at risk of losing the approval we so strongly desire. When we need to be nice, we become a slave to others' approval and to the identity we have taken on through years of reinforcement. When a relationship is based on a condition that needs to be in place at all times, it inevitably breaks down.

A main motivator in getting into a relationship is the hope of finding someone who will accept us unconditionally for who we are, with whom we will no longer need to play the game of approval seeking. We can be ourselves, warts and all, and still be loved without fear of being punished or rejected. We can't accept something in someone that we can't accept in ourselves. Most of us possess at least some personal qualities that we haven't fully accepted. And also, it's likely that our partner, who at first seemed to find everything about us sweet, adorable, and lovable, after a while may become somewhat less accepting of us. We may have also discovered some not-so-nice aspects of theirs that have begun to concern us.

This is the point at which we might become aware of an important choice that we have to make: 1) to try to change our partner and/or ourselves; or 2) to commit to be more accepting of those parts of ourselves. Accepting another person does not mean we tolerate bad behavior. Instead, we respect the differences in our preferences, personalities, and ways of being and resist the temptation to try to change them.

In becoming more accepting of their traits, the relationship becomes more harmonious. Imagine a life in which just being yourself is enough, and there is no obligation to continuously seek approval—and being nice and being kind aren't obligations to fulfill but natural expressions of your inner nature. Imagine how being at peace with yourself would affect your relationships, all of them. It's possible. That's the magic of self-acceptance.

68.

Me or we?

Since the perpetuation of the species is the force that drives the longing for connection, it seems natural to assume that we'd be wired to get along with ease. But for many of us, that isn't the case, especially when it comes to committed partnerships. Consider that we live in a culture that continually encourages us to fulfill two contradictory mandates. The first is to honor our "true self." This message shows up in the form of slogans, advertising jingles, song titles, and even Army recruitment posters. We are urged to "Be all that you can be!" "Be true to you," "Love yourself," "Be authentic," "Be number one in your own life!" There's nothing wrong with any of these messages. In fact, if we tend to forget that there are other reasons to be on earth besides taking care of others, such reminders can save us from a life of excessive self-sacrifice.

The second mandate is relational, serving the greater good, not just one's personal desires. One of the most painful criticisms that we can hear from others is "You're selfish!" This admonition contains the message that we shouldn't care more about ourselves than we do others (particularly the "other" who is accusing us of being selfish!). There's validity to both of these perspectives. And therein lies the challenge of all relationships. They require us to fulfill two of our strongest impulses: to support the well-being of others and of ourselves as well. Most of us are predisposed towards one of these poles. If we tend towards care of self over care of others, we are likely to be attracted to our counterpart. And vice versa. Relationships with people whose tendencies complement our own enable us to fulfill our personal as well as our interpersonal needs.

In theory, this is great idea—in practice, not so much. The fear of losing ourselves by going too far over to the "other side" often outweighs the fear of being abandoned by others. On the other hand, for some the fear of losing others outweighs the concern about preserving individual integrity. These two types of people often manage to find each other.

Despite our attraction to those who fulfill our inclination towards greater wholeness, we may be much more attached to our innate predisposition than we realize, creating a conflict within ourselves. When both partners bring this internal conflict into a relationship, the result can be an interpersonal conflict, and we're off and running, sometimes literally!

It makes sense to allow another person to support the cultivation of traits that are undeveloped, but doing so can feel dangerous. Such feelings activate controlling reactions on the part of both partners, resulting in trouble. Given the likelihood that both the internal and the interpersonal conflicts will arise when opposing desires coexist, don't be surprised if symptoms of discord show up.

Differences are distinct from conflict and don't necessarily have to lead to fighting. The challenge is to resist the temptation to win an argument in order to have our view prevail. When we accept that there is validity to our partner's orientation, we can appreciate the value their predisposition brings to our life. When one person stops coercing another to agree that their way is "correct," there is an increase in feelings of safety, which enables both partners to speak and listen with greater mutual respect.

Moving from conflict to appreciation is possible even for couples who have been trapped in cycles of resentment for years. This requires recognition of the true nature of the problem—seeing that it's not about right or wrong but about a failure to recognize the gifts each partner brings. It also requires a willingness to forgive the other person for being how they are. It's not about answering the question "Me or we?" but rather seeing that it's really about "me *and* we."

When we each acknowledge the gifts the other person brings to our life and express gratitude, the me and we dichotomy melts away.

Great relationships require interdependence *and* self-reliance. These two qualities are *not* mutually exclusive: they can and must exist simultaneously if a relationship is to truly thrive. And who knows; our partner may be just the one to help to make that happen!

69.

Flooding

Flooding is the feeling of being overwhelmed by powerful emotions. Feelings are not determined by logic or reason and are not predictable. We can't help but feel whatever we feel in any given situation. When we experience a loss, we may feel sad. When we believe that we are being treated unjustly, we may feel indignant. When we are pleasantly surprised, we feel delighted. Feelings come uninvited; they just come.

There are times when feelings come with such strength that we may become unable to respond rationally. Feelings can also come in clusters of differing emotions simultaneously. Confusion, anger, and frustration can occur together, as can guilt, remorse, and sadness, or shame, fear, and unworthiness.

When we are subject to emotions that arise simultaneously, it can feel like we're temporarily insane, and in some ways we are. Our normal thought process has been hijacked by our emotions and we're no longer in our right mind. We have all, at one time or another, been possessed by powerful emotional states that temporarily take us over. Some experience this only on rare occasions. For others, the feeling of being overwhelmed is constant.

There will inevitably be times when we are caught in the grip of emotional possession. We will experience such an intense desire to escape that we find ourselves doing anything we can be free of it. Any choices we make while in this state will be misguided, since they will arise out of our distorted emotions. Consequently, most of our reactions aggravate the situation.

Unless we interrupt this cycle, we will go into a full-blown state of panic, which doesn't help. Only when we cool our inflamed emotions can we free ourselves from the grip of being flooded.

This process involves the following:

- Feel the feeling. Locate the place of overwhelm where it exists in the body to experience the sensation of being flooded.
- Identify the feeling. Choose a word or phrase, such as *flooded, overwhelmed, triggered, possessed,* or whatever comes to mind.
- Acknowledge to yourself that you have gone into an altered state. Doing so allows you to be where you are rather than indulging the tendency to get away from the experience instead of accepting its reality. Responding to the feeling will come later.
- Communicate your feelings. Inform your partner of your current state. Redirect your attention away from them as the source of your emotional state.
- Consider taking a time-out. If you need one, it isn't necessary to ask for permission.

Feeling overwhelmed is nobody's fault. Blaming the other person isn't dishonest; it just isn't accurate. They have touched a tender place, which activated an unhealed wound that triggered intense emotions. In the midst of the fray, it's difficult to maintain clearheadedness. But it is possible, with time, effort, and practice, to get back on track after being derailed. We can't stop the waves from coming, but we can learn to surf.

70.

From avoidance to engagement

Conflict avoidance is a habit that generally begins in childhood, often as a result of anxiety that originated in painful interactions within one's family. It is a strategy to secure safety by speaking or acting in ways that prevent the provocation of hostile responses. There are, however, significant costs to maintaining the habit of avoidance:

- An inability to engage authentically with others
- The promotion of feelings of helplessness, hopelessness, and resentment
- The reinforcement of passivity and feelings of being victimized
- A diminishment of feelings of happiness, enthusiasm, and gratitude
- A loss of self-respect and the respect of others
- A loss of feelings of connection particularly in one's intimate relationships

The good news is that recovery from conflict avoidance is possible, even for those who have been avoiders for years or even decades. Here are some guidelines:

- Fess up. Being a conflict avoider is nothing to be ashamed of.
- Practice self-forgiveness for all the times you have judged yourself because you felt ashamed.

- Forgive others towards whom you have harbored resentment. If you don't feel ready to do so, forgive yourself for not being ready yet.
- Take responsibility for your part in the creation of your conflict-phobia. Doing so does not relieve others of their responsibility.
- If you feel that an apology is warranted, express what you feel regretful about.
- Declare your intention to clean up the difficulties your avoidance has caused.
- Thank your partner for joining you in bringing greater trust and honesty into your relationship.

Chances are the issues will not be completely resolved by one conversation. End the conversation by saying, "To be continued." With gentle and committed persistence, defensive patterns, even those that have been in place for a long time, can be neutralized into interchanges that transform previously deadlocked stalemates. It's never too early or too late to begin the process!

71.

Sore spots

Sore spots. Everyone has them: those places where we get easily triggered, quickly defensive, and irrationally reactive. It's the emotional equivalent of being poked in a fresh wound. Those unhealed places that haven't yet received sufficient care remind us that they need more loving attention and perhaps forgiveness, or maybe just time. Some of us may be fortunate enough to have just a few of them; others have more, sometimes a lot more. We'll know when we bump into a sore spot. Our partner will let us know, but they probably won't signal with an "Ouch!" or politely say, "Excuse me, but I think you just bumped into one of my sore spots." They might get angry and yell. Or they might go silent and moody. Or cry. Or say, "Nothing" when you ask them, "What's wrong?" And we'll probably react similarly when we're the one who gets triggered. It feels safer to withdraw, get angry, or just not talk about it because revealing that we feel hurt or scared means being vulnerable.

Activating sore spots in others and getting activated ourselves isn't a question of "if"; it's a matter of "when." Because few, if any, of us are completely free of them, we're going to be both the triggered and the triggerer from time to time. Sore spots originate in early life experiences (frequently in childhood) when we felt too much shame or fear to acknowledge our pain or were at risk of being punished. The overt or covert message came as "How could you be so stupid?" or "What's wrong with you?" Neither of these are questions but are actually condemnations. They can be experienced as threats or curses, such as "I'm ashamed of you" or "I can't take this any longer," "You're just like your father," or "You're selfish."

It could also be related to a physical characteristic about which we feel shame, or an accusation concerning something about our personality that we fear repulses others. It can be painful when anyone, particularly someone close to us, touches our sore places. We react by bracing ourselves for attack. Although our partner did not cause the pain, it can seem like they did. They merely activated pain lying beneath the surface of our awareness that was already present but not completely healed. In committed relationships, we can count on our partner to activate any areas that need healing.

Like the saying goes, we can see this experience as a problem or an opportunity. The opportunity is the possibility of bringing attention to the old fear, shame, anger, or grief. Rather than reacting with anger at another for causing us pain, or at ourselves for hurting, we are called upon to bring a quality of presence that promotes healing. Here are the stages that characterize this process:

- Awareness: By becoming aware of our sore places, we can identify the limiting beliefs we adopted long ago. Facing these beliefs is essential to the healing process.
- Curiosity: This is about becoming interested in what we are actually experiencing rather than "shooting the messenger" who brings us the news.
- Responsibility: Until we rise up to a higher level of ownership of our areas of sensitivity, we will continue to project fault onto others. Projection reinforces the belief that we are powerless to do anything about our situation.
- Support: When we turn our attention to our wounds that need compassionate attention rather than blame our partner for touching them, the real healing begins.
- Vulnerability: Letting our partner know exactly what we are feeling enables them to understand what we need from them. It can be as simple as wanting them to be more sensitive to whatever issue was activated.

By providing respectful responses, the cycles of reactivity gradually become replaced with enhanced trust. The patterns being challenged have probably been in place for many years, even decades, and it's unlikely that they will quickly give way to nondefensive responses. But with persistence, they do give way. When we feel the relief that comes from finally being freed from the obsolete programs that have been dominating our life, there's no going back!

72.

If you don't want her to be a nag, treat her like a thoroughbred.

Charlie: No one likes to be nagged, and no one likes to be a nag. Having been on the receiving end of what I used to refer to as Linda's nagging, it was no fun to be constantly reminded of things that I had agreed to do but hadn't yet done. My response would generally be a justification, which didn't relieve either Linda's frustration or my resentment for being treated like a child. Our reactions and counterreactions to each other served to more deeply entrench each of us in these feelings.

It was easy for us to see ourselves as victims of the other's wrongdoing. It's much easier to recognize what the other person is doing wrong than it is to become aware of our own part in the scenario. It's easier for the nagger to see why the other person needs to be reprimanded, and for the naggee to feel justified in responding with anger. Such responses, however, do little to address the underlying issues and usually serve to further erode things.

There are needs that are not being fulfilled, leaving one person feeling unseen, unheard, or neglected and the other feeling guilty, harassed, controlled, or irritated. At first glance, it may appear that the nagger is more to blame for the ill will that both partners have towards each other. Upon closer examination, it becomes evident that the breakdown is an imbalance in the relationship system itself.

The unpleasant emotions each partner feels are not being caused by either person but rather by a failure of both partners to respond to each other with consideration. Something has become more important to each of them than the quality of the relationship. Examples of such competing commitments include the desire to acquire or maintain control ("No one is going to tell me what to do"), the desire to prevent disappointment, an effort to obtain a superior position, or a desire to avoid feelings of guilt and shame.

Simply bringing up a relationship issue can be considered nagging by some people. The way the issue is presented, particularly whether it is accusatory, significantly impacts the response to the complainer's concern. When the conversation is initiated without accusation, the cycle of nagging and defensiveness becomes avoidable. Since the desire to fulfill an unmet need causes one partner to repeatedly address an issue until that need is met, the cycle will continue to repeat itself. Attending to the need underlying the complaint will dissolve the complaint.

When we get curious and seek to lean into rather than withdraw from the situation, things begin to change. Bringing genuine interest enables us to ask questions that can transform an impasse into a breakthrough, such as "What is it that you need from me right now?" As a more respectful connection becomes established, the kinds of action steps that will deepen trust become evident. Both partners have responsibility for implementing these steps. Doing so is a labor of love, not one of obligation. The shift comes when one person listens deeply to the other's concerns and commits to doing their best to come up with a solution that will leave both feeling acknowledged. This commitment becomes easier when there is a clear awareness that any solution that doesn't leave both partners satisfied is no solution at all.

Whether we view our circumstance as a curse or a blessing is entirely up to each of us. As we see the possibilities that arise out of a willingness to embrace rather than rail against our situation, it becomes increasingly difficult to keep our hearts closed. The nagging cycle is finally over. May it rest in peace.

73.

Honesty

It may seem like honesty is such an obvious ingredient in all relationships that it should go without saying how important it is. Yet over the years, we never fail to be surprised at the frequency with which we find couples being dishonest with each other. They find ways to justify their dishonesty, often without any conscious awareness of the consequences of doing so.

Many of these people are so accustomed to rationalizing this behavior that they don't recognize that they are being dishonest with themselves and/or others. They, like many of us, use euphemisms and terms such as *fib, white lie, misspeak, exaggeration,* or *alternative fact* to the list of lies to obscure the fact that they are intentionally attempting to create a false impression.

Some of the more popular ways of justifying dishonesty include telling ourselves that we don't want to hurt others' feelings, or that it's no big deal, or everybody does it, or it's not going to do any harm, or it would be worse if we *did* tell the truth.

The reality is that lying, whatever we call it, does cause harm, although that harm isn't always immediately evident. But sooner or later, its consequences will show up in the form of a diminishment of trust and affection, and increased feelings of anxiety, resentment and guilt.

Dishonesty can come in many forms and isn't limited to statements that are untrue. Any time we are operating from a conscious intention to mislead, we are engaging in dishonest communication. And sometimes the lie is not what we are saying; it's what we are not saying.

For example, in a relationship in which one partner chooses not to disclose information that was relevant to the relationship in order to withhold something that could be upsetting, they are engaging in a deceptive practice. "I didn't exactly lie, I just didn't tell all the details" is what we often hear from those who are attempting to defend such actions.

One of the most frequent types of honesty that characterizes great relationships is emotional honesty. While factual honesty has to do with stating things such as "I have blue eyes" or "There are thirty-one days in July" or "My cat's name is Snowflake," emotional honesty has to do with the expression of feelings that arise out of an interpersonal interaction, such as "I'm disappointed that you forgot my birthday" or "I'm grateful to you for helping me out in the garden" or "When you called me a lazy slob, I felt hurt and angry."

While we don't have to share every single emotion that we feel, there are times when the failure to honestly express our feelings can be problematic, particularly when failing to do so creates a false impression.

During the early years of our relationship I (Linda) was guilty of withholding many feelings that I had towards Charlie out of fear that revealing them might cause an upset, something that I very much wanted to prevent. The primary feeling I withheld from him was anger. I was afraid that expressing myself would activate *his* anger and that I would be no match for him. I had spent my childhood withholding my feelings since expressing many of them would have provoked severe consequences, particularly from my father.

When Charlie and I first got together, my level of truth telling was not very high. I had taken the role of the peacemaker in my family and was experienced at covering up my distress and anger in an attempt to avoid the explosions that were commonplace in my home.

Early in our relationship, Charlie put me on notice that such posturing did not work for him. He told me often when I told him that I was fine, he knew that I wasn't. He also said that he considered it dishonest for me to insist that everything was fine with me when, in truth, it wasn't. Charlie sensed that beneath my smiling face, something was brewing. Feeling like the kid caught with her hand in the cookie jar, I sheepishly admitted, "Well, maybe not *everything* is fine."

And that began one of the most powerful conversations we had ever had. We both ended up getting very vulnerable and emotionally honest with each other. Charlie made it clear to me how crucial it was to him that we have what he referred to as a "no-bullshit relationship." He told me that although his parents had their problems, just as mine did, one of the things he learned while growing up was that a relationship that wasn't emotionally honest wasn't worth having, and that even truths that are hard to hear need to be spoken if they are relevant to the relationship. His bottom line, he told me, was that if we didn't have that agreement, it would be a deal-breaker for him.

I was already crazy about Charlie and wanted our relationship to last a lifetime. I was in terror of the idea of having to bring up the tough issues, especially my anger and my unmet needs, but I was more afraid of losing our relationship and having to live without him. I heard the steely truth in Charlie's voice and I knew he meant what he said. It was a turning point in my life and in our relationship and the beginning of a new, and steep, learning curve for me in which I practiced, certainly not perfectly, doing and saying things that I had spent my whole life repressing and even denying to myself. It was very hard, particularly early on, but over time, I became what I referred to as a warrior of the heart. That is, someone who pits herself not against an external enemy but against the forces within her that oppose her commitment to the authenticity and empowerment that true love calls for.

Since then, I have had thousands of opportunities to practice and to develop new ways of being. Charlie has had his own learning curve to deal with as well. His work had to do with toning down his intensity, which could sometimes be unnecessarily harsh. We have each had to learn how to be honest with each other with respect and consideration, and to learn how to speak without blame and judgment.

This transformative process has been an essential ingredient not only in the success of our partnership but also in my sense of myself. I feel that through it all, I have grown into a person of greater integrity. I am deeply grateful to Charlie for holding a high standard about the crucial importance of honesty. And I am also grateful that he hung in there with me while we practiced together to become proficient. Of everything we have learned and accomplished over our five-plus decades of marriage, the teaching about honesty stands at the very top of the list!

74.

When "I'm sorry" just isn't enough

Since we are all mistake-prone, it behooves us to become adept in the art of making effective repairs when our relationship needs them. Try as we may, it's inevitable that there will be times when our best efforts to communicate with kindness will fall short of our intended outcome. There will also be times when we say or do things when we're possessed by strong emotions that may cause harm to another, and we find ourselves feeling remorse and wishing for a do-over. The best way to put in a correction for a regrettable communication is often through an apology.

Making an effective apology is both an art and a science. Here are some conditions to consider to help you get back on track:

- Sincerity: Make sure that your apology is heartfelt. The word *sincere* means "clean, pure, free from falsehood or pretense." Don't bother saying anything until you really mean it.
- Timing: Timing is important in terms of the other person's readiness to receive your apology. If they are still too hurt or angry, it's better to wait until they are more receptive.
- Intentionality: Don't use an apology manipulatively to shut another person up. Check your intention to make sure that you really are committed to healing the breakdown.
- Vulnerability: Try not to indulge in justifications. Disarm yourself of any defensiveness.

- Vision: Hold a vision of what you hope for as a result of your dialogue.
- Be specific: Avoid generalizations and specify what it is that you regret having done or said that caused the other person pain. "I'm sorry that you feel that way" is not an apology.
- Responsibility: Admit that you made a regrettable choice (for example, broke an agreement, made a hurtful remark, spoke in a threatening or condescending tone). Acknowledge your transgression without justifying your actions. Although a one-time sincere apology may be sufficient, serious wounds sometimes require multiple apologies.
- Make amends: Clear up the damage you caused to restore things to the condition they were in prior to the breakdown.
- Commitment: Tell your partner that you are committed to doing your best to prevent similar future occurrences.
- Reassurance: Let the other person know that you have learned an important lesson from this experience and tell them what it is.
- Request forgiveness: If the other person is not yet ready to forgive you, respect their response and thank them for their honesty. Declare that you will hang in there until they trust you as much as you trust yourself to fulfill your promises.
- Patience: Your partner may need to express their disappointment or other feelings before they can be fully present to receive your apology. Try to resist the temptation to "set the record straight."
- Gratitude: Thank your partner for being open to joining you in restoring goodwill back into your relationship.

When we have confidence that harm caused through unskillful choices can be fully healed, we become motivated to use the methods that we know work to keep our relationship in the best possible condition. Successful apologies can not only restore our relationship to its pre-breakdown condition but also take it to higher levels of trust and understanding than it previously had. A sincere apology can go a long way!

75.

Forgiveness

Forgiveness has to do with making a conscious choice to relinquish resentment resulting from a real or perceived injury. Although it may be the most important tool in our relationship tool kit, it is one of the most underutilized. Letting go of grudges can be difficult because relinquishing these feelings leaves us open to the risk of getting re-wounded. Holding resentment can feel safer than letting it go because it seems to provide us with an extra layer of protection.

Forgiveness does not require us to forget the experience. Forgiveness frees us from the prison of our preoccupation with a past wounding. It is as much a gift to ourselves as it is to the other person. Sincere forgiveness cannot be provided through coercion; it must be freely given Forgiveness is generally not a single event but rather a process that occurs over time, sometimes needing multiple repetitions to create a true sense of completion.

We can't force ourselves or anyone else to forgive, but we can set the conditions that will predispose us towards an inclination to forgive. We can remind ourselves of why we want to forgive, who we feel the need to forgive, from whom we feel a desire to be forgiven, and remind ourselves of what we stand to gain by letting go of resentment.

Separating the truth about forgiveness from fictitious beliefs about it can hasten the process. What follows is a series of guidelines for living a life of greater peace and understanding. Consider them when you feel the call to forgive.

- Forgiveness in no way excuses the person who caused harm or in any way justifies their actions.
- Forgiveness is an inside job. It doesn't necessarily require a confrontation with another person.
- Forgiveness is always a choice. You do *not* have to forgive.
- You don't forgive just for the sake of others but for the sake of your own peace of mind.
- Forgiveness is not a moral obligation but a practical gift to yourself and others.
- The act of forgiving enhances one's sense of self-worth.
- You may forgive someone and still choose to keep your distance from them.
- Try to forgive yourself when you don't feel ready to forgive.

Forgiveness is an act of love that opens our heart and enhances our sense of wholeness. The more we forgive, the more we strengthen life-affirming qualities, including (but not limited to) compassion, patience, integrity, humility, and personal power. There may be no other single practice that can provide so much for us and others. Each act of forgiveness liberates us from grievances that diminish our quality of well-being. It is truly the gift that keeps on giving.

76.

Don't bring out the big guns.

Sometimes in an argument, a fear of loss will cause one partner to bring out the big guns and start waving them in the air out of desperation. Big guns are implicit or explicit threats, often of separation, divorce, or abandonment. Statements like "You are impossible to deal with," "I'm done with this relationship," "I've had it with you and your hysterics. I'm outta here!" or "If a divorce is what you want, you can have it!"

The impulse to intimidate, bully, or threaten someone often arises in a person who is experiencing intense anxiety. These threats are often delivered in an effort to intimidate the other person into accommodating demands or to disarm them.

While most of us have, at times, felt this kind of desperation and may have even made threats, the damage these big guns can cause is often far greater than either partner realizes. This is not to suggest that conversations about separation or divorce should be prohibited. Rather they should be discussed only when cooler heads prevail and the conversation can be grounded in rational communication rather than as a manifestation of fear or rage. Divorce used as a threat, particularly if it is presented in a context of intense emotional reactivity, can make that outcome more likely.

When a couple's conflict gets overheated, and the threat of divorce is made, it creates a huge disturbance. That threat is the ultimate weapon, the nuclear option that puts the other person on notice that we've reached the very end of our bandwidth and that something's got to give!

Such messages do not predispose things to go well. The person who is the target of ultimatums is hard pressed to stay open to negotiate in good faith. Strong-arm tactics only result in fear-based behavior. Even if the intimidator succeeds in getting his or her way, the victory comes with a huge price tag. The hurt and resentment that accrue as a result of such threats is great and can significantly destabilize the relationship on a long-term basis.

Trust can be damaged to such a degree that it may take weeks or even months to be adequately repaired. Although these threats are made in an attempt to intimidate, the result is often just the opposite. The targeted person may counterattack with threats of their own, which often results in escalations in the intensity of the interaction. Consequently, it's best to do everything in our power to eliminate, or at least minimize, the introduction of the big guns into the conversation. Here are a few suggestions:

- Learn to use your words to express what you feel and what you need rather than weaponizing them against your partner
- Cultivate the art of emotional vulnerability .
- Get some good help and hold the vision that it is possible to find a way through the difficult times to establish a working partnership.
- Practice forgiveness.

Do these things for your own sake, for the sake of the relationship, and for the sake of everyone you love. You'll never regret it. Guaranteed!

77.

Confessions of a recovering helper

Charlie: The other day I caught myself feeling like a victim. Again. I've been writing and teaching about responsibility long enough to know that whenever I feel victimized by someone or something, there's usually (like, about 99 percent of the time) something for me to learn. This particular instance was no exception. I was feeling overloaded, overtired, and resentful, all of which I've come to recognize as symptoms of putting more on my plate than is really good for me.

Admittedly, part of me is attached to seeing myself as a good guy who can be there for anyone, anytime. You could say that I'm a recovering helper. And I've even got a graduate degree to prove it! As a very experienced helper, I'm generally pretty mindful of the symptoms of over-giving. They include the three that I just mentioned, as well as feeling irritable, grumpy, and holding on to unresolved grievances.

Fortunately, in recent years I've become acutely aware of these symptoms when they (less frequently than in the past) show up and hijack my normally good mood. When I recognize the part I play in creating these feelings, I can put in the corrections that bring me back to "normal." These days it doesn't take too long, usually no more than a few hours. Sometimes, it's just a matter of minutes before I'm back to being "myself" again.

I currently live in a mood of gratitude almost all of the time, which makes it a lot more pleasant for those who are around me and for me to be around myself. That's probably why I am so quick to notice when I'm feeling grumpy.

The most frequent correction to over-giving is to give myself a healthy dose of responsible self-care. I put a temporary moratorium on placing anything that isn't absolutely necessary on my plate. I renegotiate agreements that are stressing me out, forgive myself for slipping into the black hole again, and apologize to anyone I may have offended.

For me, apologizing is not about admitting to a transgression in order to receive forgiveness but rather a means through which I acknowledge responsibility for my actions. This relieves others of any concern that they were at fault for my responses to them, and provides me some relief for any guilt I experience.

While the other person may also bear some responsibility if there has been a breakdown between us, it is their business to deal with that and not mine to point it out to them. In acknowledging my responsibility, I affirm to myself the consequences of my actions, thereby driving home the lesson that I need to learn in order to minimize the likelihood of repeating this pattern. Entrenched habits don't die quickly or easily, but with practice and clear intentionality, they do diminish over time. They show up with less and less frequency, and they are neutralized more quickly.

I don't know if I'll ever be completely free of the impulse to default to feelings of self-pity and irritability when I overload myself, but for me that's no longer the point. Knowing what I need to do to minimize the eruption of these tendencies and putting practices in place that will prevent them from taking my generally positive attitude hostage for very long is good enough for me. And who knows, maybe I'll get lucky and find that I can totally remove my impulse to over-give. I'm not too hopeful about that one. But anything's possible!

78.

Are you talking about money or fighting about it?

It doesn't take a rocket scientist or a professional researcher to know that one of the top things couples fight about is money. Strangely, money also tops the list of topics that couples need to but don't talk about enough. In case this seems contradictory to you, let us explain. Money can be a loaded subject, and because we have had few stress-free conversations about it, we are understandably reluctant when it comes to this subject. Hence there is a tendency to put conversations about money on the back burner.

When we move things to the back burner, they tend to get neglected, even though the burner is still on, and it's not until we start to smell something burning that we turn our attention to the source of the smell. By that time, we may have a fire to put out. Rather than having a civil conversation, we find ourselves in emergency mode and ill equipped to communicate skillfully. Consequently, the outcome of our interaction is unlikely to be productive, and our desire to avoid future conversations about finances is even greater. This creates a vicious cycle of denial, frustration, avoidance, and arguing.

You are probably wondering how to break this cycle, or whether it's even possible to break it. These are good questions, but the more immediate question is why money is such a loaded issue for so many, and why just talking about it can trigger such powerful feelings.

We live in a culture which places a very high value on material goods. Money provides access to the things that have personal and social value. Money is also regarded as the means through which our own value is assessed by others, and even by ourselves, enabling us to obtain abstractions such as power, influence, worthiness, and security. While some of us tend to be more possessed by these shared cultural views than others, we all have had to deal with them. With so much on the line, it's no wonder that the topic of money is such a hot button for so many.

Adding to this mix, we all bring our own personal history, and future goals. It's a wonder that more relationships don't collapse under the weight of it all. It seems like an accident waiting to happen!

And yet as daunting as the challenge to navigate this minefield can appear to be, some couples do manage to pool their collective personal resources (assets and liabilities) and succeed in co-creating a good life.

Here are a few of the things we've learned from those couples:

- Communication: Practice good communication. If you lack the necessary skills, learn, practice, and develop them. Get the support you need in order to become a champion listener and an effective speaker.
- Responsibility: Quit the blame game and focus on what you can do to be a more skillful agent in your conversations about money.
- Vision: Dedicate yourselves to the fulfillment of a joint vision.
- Support: Be willing to solicit, receive, and act upon guidance of those who you deem to be more knowledgeable about finances than you are. Join or create a network of mutual support with others who share your vision of money management.
- Prioritize: Seek to create alignment with your partner regarding priorities and values.
- Self-discipline: Practice restraint when it comes to impulse buying and remind yourself how good it will feel to live a life that is more guilt-free with greater peace of mind.
- Creativity: Collaborate and use your imagination to come up with ways of bringing more pleasure into your life with experiences that require little or no expense.

These are some of the many things we can do that will have a lasting impact on our ability to face the more challenging aspects of finance-related conversations.

79.

Don't be a SAP (speculations, assumptions, and projection).

Charlie: The word *project* has multiple definitions and two possible pronunciations. The noun form has an emphasis on the first syllable, as in "Writing this book has been a fascinating and challenging project." The verb has the emphasis on the second syllable, as in "Sometimes I get so frustrated with the process that I want to project my laptop out the window."

In this chapter we'll be talking about project as a thing and project as an action—more specifically, a psychological action. One of the dictionary definitions is "to transfer or attribute one's own emotion or desire to another person, especially unconsciously."

Projection occurs in all relationships. When we believe we know what our partner wants or needs, or what their mood is, we are projecting our own experience onto them. Our assumptions are, as the dictionary reminds us, unconscious—based on a projection of what we think we would be experiencing if we were in their shoes. We are not only unaware that we are doing this and acting in accordance with our assumptions, but we are also unaware that our assumptions may be inaccurate.

The sad fact of the matter is that most of what we think we know about another person's current needs, thoughts, feelings, and desires isn't necessarily accurate. Unfortunately, many of us hold our speculations as "the truth" and rarely question them even in the face of significant evidence to the contrary, like when they react to our well-intended "support" with anger, hurt feelings, or bewilderment.

Here's a personal example: In the early days of our relationship, before Linda and I had learned much about psychology, we would get into "misunderstandings." And sometimes they would get overheated—sometimes highly so. At this point we would react to what was rapidly becoming a meltdown by trying to "fix" the other person, who we were each convinced was at fault and needed to change. We assumed that we knew what they needed from us.

This assumption was based on what we ourselves wanted at the time. And if we both had identical personalities, things would have worked out fine.. As it was, that was not the case. Not only were our personalities *not* identical, but they are in many ways polar opposites.

Linda tends towards the touchy-feely, extroversion side of the spectrum, while I am on the introverted, cerebral side of it. She wanted to get warm and fuzzy and do some serious talking. So, she "knew" that was what I must need too. She reasoned that if I wasn't sufficiently in touch with my need for closeness, she would help me by getting closer, which was what she believed any "normal" person would need.

Meanwhile, my reaction to her bids for more connection was to withdraw with an intense desire to take a time-out, a long one. Each of us was desperately trying to pull the other person over to our preferred position, which caused the other to push harder for their position.

We were both trying to give each other the very last thing the other person wanted because we had each projected our own desires onto them. The outcome was not pretty. Fortunately, we did finally manage to recognize the flaw in our assumptions. Linda saw it before I did, and she patiently hung in there until I, slow learner that I am, eventually got it.

And the "it" that I eventually got was that it's not a good idea to believe everything I think. That doesn't mean I should disbelieve whatever I think, but since I can't stop my projections from coming, I can at least learn to recognize them for what they are: speculations that emerge from my own mind that may or may not be accurate.

The truth is that I really can't know for sure what is going on within another person unless I have more to go on than my own ideas, which tend to be biased. When I remember this, I become more curious, less certain, but also interested in finding out what is actually going on with them rather than confusing my imaginings with "reality." I become less attached to a position that may be inhibiting my ability to get to know the person in front of me, and more likely to discover who they are in the moment.

Then it becomes possible to see, accept, and even appreciate the reality that we each inhabit. This is the only place in which true understanding and meaningful connection can occur. When we can clear the field of any assumptions that obstruct our ability to see "what is," we are positioned to work together in a shared reality as partners, not adversaries. And from this place, anything is possible. Anything.

80.

Ten magic words

Mira and Joel had a problem—or as she put it, an opportunity. It seemed that Joel was afflicted with that not-so-rare condition that many men, and a fair number of women, are possessed by, sometimes known as "Here's what you need to do-itis." It's where one partner begins expressing feelings such as frustration, confusion, anxiety, or disappointment about a concern they have. Before they even finish expressing themselves, their partner has jumped in, interrupting them with some advice that they believe to be a sure-fire solution to the problem. If you have been on the receiving end of this pattern, you probably know where this is going.

Mira and Joel found themselves in this situation quite frequently, and each time, things always went the same way. Joel would offer his words of wisdom within seconds of Mira initiating the conversation. Mira would then stop talking, allowing him to finish telling her what she needed to do to "fix" the situation. Then he would not-so-patiently wait for her to thank him for his words of wisdom and to reassure him that she would do what he had suggested. Mira resented Joel's frequent advice but chose to silently tolerate it in order to avoid making him angry.

She stated that Joel didn't like it when his advice wasn't followed. When she was more honest with him—for example, telling him that she had no intention of accepting his advice—he would get angry or sullen, which left her feeling upset.

Mira: "When I shared my concerns with Joel, I was hoping to lighten my load. It quickly got turned around, and I ended up feeling that now I had to take care of him so that he didn't get upset. I never got what I really wanted, and I usually ended up feeling disappointed and frustrated. Still, I kept my mouth shut and tried to just suck it up to be a good girl, like I learned to be as a kid. One day, I exploded in the middle of one of Joel's long-winded directives. 'Will you just shut up?' I screamed, shocking Joel and myself as well. To my surprise, Joel went silent. There was a long pause, and then he finally said, 'What's wrong with you?'"

"'I'm sorry,' I said, apologizing like a good girl should when she has lost her temper, which she is never supposed to do. But immediately after that, a stream of frustration over all of the times I should have spoken up came pouring out. I had reached the limit of what I could contain. All my pent-up anger, not only at Joel but at myself, came out. Probably if I had been more honest during those previous times when I stuffed my feelings, that explosion wouldn't have occurred. There would have been some milder interactions rather than one major blowup. But in a way, I'm glad that it did come to a head because out of that situation, Joel and I had a 'come to Jesus' meeting that broke the cycle that we had been in for years."

From that meeting, and those that followed, Joel and Mira took some necessary steps in breaking the pattern in which they had been locked for much of their marriage. Mira informed him that when he offered his unsolicited advice, she felt that he was talking down to her as though she were a little girl and he was the wise parent giving her the benefit of his sage wisdom.

Mira: "I usually don't want your advice. I just want you to listen to me. Sometimes I really do want your advice, and when I do, I will ask for it. But I never get a chance to ask because you always rush in, telling me what you think I need to do. It makes me feel small and inferior to you. You seemed so upset when I didn't take your advice that I decided it wasn't worth it to let you know how I really felt. I decided to pretend to go along with you, but inside I knew that I wouldn't. I'm sorry for not being more honest with you."

Joel: "I appreciate your apology, and I would rather hear the truth than to have you pretend you are listening to me when you aren't."

Mira: "That's what I want too, for you to just listen to me and let me get things off my chest. But it seemed like you wanted me to do what you wanted me to do."

Joel: "I guess we both wanted the same thing: to be heard, to feel connected, and to feel each other's support. Actually, I often do want you to take my advice. I hate to see you suffering. And I do think that if you would only accept my guidance, you would feel better. And the truth is, it does make me feel good when you find my advice helpful."

Mira: "And sometimes I do value your perspective, but sometimes what I want more than that is just for you to give me the time to express my feelings."

Joel: "Well, how am I supposed to know whether you want my advice or just for me to listen to you?"

Mira: "I'll tell you when I want advice, and if I don't request it, just assume that I don't want it."

Joel: "Okay. But you know this habit of offering you my brilliant wisdom is pretty ingrained in me, so I might slip and give it sometimes even if you don't ask. Then what?"

Mira: "Is it okay for me to tell you that I just want you to listen?"

Joel: "Yeah. I think that I can handle that without feeling crushed. And if I do, I'll get over it."

Mira: "I know you will, and I'll feel a whole lot better and more appreciative of your input if you give me a chance to ask for it."

Joel: "Then it's a deal."

They kiss.

And those ten magic words? "If I want your advice, I'll ask you for it."

81.

The high cost of nursing a grudge

"Holding a grudge is like swallowing poison and expecting someone else to die."

—Anonymous

Bob and Lydia, a middle-aged couple, had been married for almost twenty years when they came for counseling. They were both in agreement that their marriage was in rough shape and that they should have gotten counseling long ago. What they were not in agreement about was the reason things were so broken down. Like many troubled couples, they each placed the blame for the breakdown on the other person.

Although they claimed the issue was their finances, it soon became clear that money was a symptom, not the source of the problem. Their family had been living on the financial margins throughout their marriage. Lydia had a full-time job that provided a modest, reliable income. Bob was in business for himself but had been unable to achieve the degree of success that he and Lydia had hoped for. With four kids, they were always scrambling to make ends meet.

When Lydia's father died, leaving her an inheritance, she decided to invest the money in real estate. Bob was disappointed because he preferred that Lydia use the money as a down payment for the purchase of a home. Although he acknowledged that it was Lydia's money and she had a right to do what she wanted, Bob was angry about her decision. Over time, Bob's anger turned in a grudge that he nursed by obsessively thinking about how deprived he felt the family was because of what he considered to be Lydia's selfishness.

Although the couple never discussed either of their feelings about her investment, Lydia began to sense that not all was okay with Bob. He was growing increasingly more irritable with her and the kids. He was also becoming sullen and withdrawn. Inwardly Bob felt embarrassed for not being a better provider, and his anger covered his deeper feelings of shame.

Meanwhile their relationship slowly spiraled downhill. Lydia dealt with the deterioration of their marriage by becoming more involved with her work and her real estate investments. She found herself feeling increasingly more disconnected from Bob because of his continual criticisms and what she considered to be his insufficient financial contributions to the family. She also didn't trust him financially, due to years of mismanagement of his business.

Over time, their relationship became increasingly distant, cold, and bitter. Because Bob continually reaffirmed his grudges against Lydia, and because she refused to be honest about Bob's failure to be more financially responsible, the situation deteriorated to the point that their mutual insults became overt.

Bob knew that he was in pain, but he was unaware that his attachment to his vindictive resentment was the major cause of his suffering. His obsessive dwelling on his anger toward Lydia deepened his conviction that she was the cause of his misery. He saw himself as an innocent victim. Bob felt entitled to share control of the money that Lydia had inherited, despite the fact that he had not earned her trust that he would make wise financial decisions. Lydia's failure to express her concerns about Bob's financial judgment prevented an honest conversation that might have opened the possibility of taking constructive action.

Although it may be uncomfortable, it's possible at any time to bring up difficult subjects. A failure to do so when such action needs to be taken can result in serious damage to a relationship. Sometimes the person holding the grudge will deliberately provoke others into opposition because that fuels his or her fury. Bob was attached to his view of things as the correct one. Period. He only wanted to justify his anger and was not open to reason. When Lydia did try to speak in her own behalf, he accused her of trying to control his life.

In time, Lydia reached a point where she became more able to tell Bob that she was unwilling to be blamed any longer, and she eventually moved out. Even today, years later, Bob is still unable to see the connection between his pain and grudge holding. Until he does, he's likely to continue to perpetuate this dreadful cycle even though he rarely has any contact with Lydia. Until Bob accepts responsibility for his contribution to his pain, he will continue to see himself as a helpless victim of a mean-spirited woman, and will continue to reinforce that perception by dwelling on angry thoughts about her.

What finally interrupts this cycle and brings relief is acceptance, responsibility, understanding and compassion for oneself and others. Even decades-long grudges can melt away when we bring these qualities more fully into our lives.

Grudges tend to expand to the point where resentment leaks out in the form of spiteful words and a bitter attitude. Bob sought revenge for the hurt that he felt Lydia had done to him. Unconsciously, he moved through the three stages of grudge holding. He moved out of stage one, where the resentment is concealed, to stage two, expressing insulting remarks, and then into stage three in his disrespectful behaviors and emotional disengagement from Lydia. Bob knew that his cold silence was the thing that hurt her the most.

The trait that the grudge holder embodies is vindictiveness. They project their self-hate onto others in an attempt to relieve some of their suffering. This misguided effort to relieve suffering creates pain both for the grudge holder and the one being blamed. Bob's failure to accept responsibility for his part in the breakdown created a vicious cycle. His desire to vindicate himself amplifies the cycle that can only be interrupted by a willingness to recognize his contribution to the impasse.

Bringing compassion both for oneself and another is the way out of the suffering. It is Bob's work to become aware that inner grudge holder is bloated with too much power. It is necessary to admit that holding grudges is a destructive pattern, and that it's not only the people "out there" who have this pattern. It's us too.

It's then that we can begin to see the prices we pay for refusing to let go of previous grievances. When we reject thoughts that continue to focus on the past, we lift off layers of pain and anger that have accumulated over the years. When we see how much lighter we feel, the new pattern takes on a life and momentum of its own.

When we realize that what our partner is bringing something that we need rather than viewing their tendency as a problem to be avoided or overruled, we begin to view them as an ally rather than an adversary. This shift in perspective radically transforms our relationship, often permanently.

82.
Connectors and freedom fighters

You may have heard of the two-step. If you think this refers to a new or old dance craze, you're right, except it's not the kind of dance that you're thinking of. It's a dance in which both partners want to take the lead, and their idea of the "correct" way to dance is the exact opposite of the other's. It's not a physical dance in which people are coordinating distance and movement with each other; it's about interpersonal intimacy and emotional connection. When Eileen McCann came out with her book *The Two Step: The Dance Toward Intimacy* in 1985, I (Linda) was instantly intrigued by the title, not just out of professional curiosity but for personal reasons as well. Charlie and I were all too familiar with this dance and had been doing a version of it for years. I was beyond frustrated, and the title alone told me enough about the book to convince me to buy it, which I did immediately.

The author referred to the two types of dancers as "pursuers" and "distancers." You might not be surprised to hear that I was the pursuer, and you can guess what Charlie was. A lot of the couples I was working with were dealing with the same issue. One partner often felt disappointed because there was not enough closeness, and the other often felt that they had an insufficient amount of separateness. These two contradictory impulses produced a vicious cycle in which the harder one partner pushed to get their desires filled, the stronger the counterreaction was. This intensified the cycle and amplified feelings of disappointment and resentment.

Because Charlie and I were driven by a commitment to our clients, and our own relationship, our motivation to break this pattern was strong. Eventually we did manage to free ourselves of its grip. And although the process of liberation was relatively simple, our experience wasn't easy.

Because we found the terms *distancer* and *pursuer* pejorative, we replaced them with "freedom-fighter" and "connector." Healthy relationships require both engagement and space. Too much of one or the other will cause an imbalance, which brings about another set of problems. Yet it seems to be instinctive that we are drawn to others who in various ways have predispositions that are different from our own. Having complementary preferences in regard to the level of closeness and the frequency and depth of connection is not a cruel trick of nature; it is a necessary condition to keep a healthy balance in our relationship.

What activates the vicious cycle is not that one or both of us gets triggered, but rather that we're both trying to do the same thing simultaneously: making an effort to get the other person to behave the way we want them to, to become more like ourselves. Whether we try to coerce them through intimidation, guilt-tripping, criticism, threats, or any other form of manipulation, these tactics only lock us more deeply into the cycle. It's only when we both stop trying to get the other person to accommodate our desire that it becomes possible to find a middle ground with which we can both live, at least for now.

These personality predispositions never go away. We deal with our irreconcilable differences for the rest of our lives. However, they need not continue to take us into the abyss. Even though Charlie and I have over time become more skilled in the art of interrupting our embedded habits, they still occasionally come up. But the frequency and intensity of our triggers has diminished enormously. And we move through them much more quickly than we did in the past.

Charlie: In the early days of our marriage, it was difficult for me to see Linda's desire for more closeness as something other than neediness. I was resistant to her efforts to get us to spend what I thought was an excessive amount of time together. At particularly low points, I would refer to her as a bottomless pit because it seemed to me that no matter how much time we spent together, it was never enough for her.

In actuality, the problem wasn't that Linda's need was insatiable but that the quality of attention I was giving her was poor. She often felt that my choice to spend time with her was motivated by a sense of obligation and that I wasn't particularly enjoying her company. Linda thought I was participating in an effort to fulfill my "duty" and get it over with. Often, she was absolutely right, but Linda didn't just want to be with me; she wanted me to *want* to be with her.

Unfortunately, the stronger her longing for us to be together, the more resistant to being with her I became. We were in a cycle that isn't easily broken as long as one's focus is on the other person. As trained psychotherapists, we both had arsenals of psychiatric diagnoses we would project onto each other. Needless to say, such pathologizing doesn't do a lot to make you more attractive to your partner.

There is a saying that you can never get enough of what you really don't want. None of us really wants someone to give to us because we have manipulated them into doing so. Attention given in response to manipulation is unsatisfying no matter how much of it we receive. Yet even the most independent of us needs genuine emotional connection. Similarly, we all have a need to be separate at times. Solitude is a state of being that allows us to self-reflect. When the need for these experiences goes unmet, we experience "dis-ease." Symptoms will make us aware that something in our lives requires attention.

The way out of the cycle Linda and I were in was to direct our attention to ourselves instead of focusing on what was wrong with each other. We also did our best to communicate our feelings and needs without holding each other responsible for meeting them. Linda began to appreciate solitude after I stopped making her wrong for her needs, and I became more appreciative of our togetherness time when she did the same thing regarding my need for separateness.

If our partner is predisposed to lean towards one side more than we are, we can strengthen the aspect of ourselves that is less developed. In the process of doing our work, we become more capable of experiencing an internal balance rather than being dependent on our partner to provide that balance we need. We create a more harmonious relationship and a more balanced life. Confronting our own less developed aspects requires the willingness to experience some discomfort. This will end when we begin to see what our partner gives us as a gift rather than as a problem. Consider the possibility that our discomfort is temporary and a small price to pay for a great benefit!

83.
Attachment, nonattachment, and detachment

In 1968 John Bowlby, a British psychoanalyst, wrote the first volume of his groundbreaking book *Attachment and Love*. In it he describes the intense distress experienced by infants who have been separated from their parents. Although Bowlby was primarily focused on understanding the nature of the infant–caregiver relationship, he believed that attachment characterized human experience from "the cradle to the grave."

Nearly twenty years later, in 1987, Cindy Hazan and Philip Shaver explored Bowlby's ideas in the context of romantic relationships. They found that the same motivational system that gives rise to the close emotional bond between parents and their children is responsible for the bond that develops between adults in emotionally intimate relationships. They noted that the relationship between infants and caregivers and the relationship between adult romantic partners share the following features:

- They feel safe when the other is nearby and responsive.
- They engage in close, intimate, bodily contact.
- They feel insecure when the other is inaccessible.
- They share discoveries with one another.
- They play with one another's facial features and exhibit a mutual fascination and preoccupation with one another.
- They engage in "baby talk."

Some people feel secure in their relationships, confident that their partners will be there for them, and are both open to depending on others and having others depend on them. The aspects that make an attachment figure "desirable" for infants, like responsiveness and availability, are the same factors adults find desirable in romantic partners. But this is not always the case. Those who are insecure may worry that others do not love them completely. These people are easily frustrated when their attachment needs go unmet. Others may experience what is referred to as an "avoidant attachment." They appear not to care too much about close relationships, preferring not to be too dependent upon other people or to have others be too dependent upon them.

In 1994, researchers Judith Feeney, Patricia Noller, and Victor Callan demonstrated that just as children use their parents as a secure base from which to explore their world, the same is true for romantic partners. Secure adults seek support from their partners when stressed and also provide support to their partners.

Just like the securely attached children who show that they are well adjusted and resilient, get along with their peers, and are well liked, securely attached adults thrive and generally enjoy partnerships characterized by longevity, trust, commitment, and interdependence.

In her book *Hold Me Tight*, the psychologist Susan Johnson speaks about the significance of secure adult attachment for a romantic partnership to thrive. She eloquently describes how when we are emotionally disconnected from our partner, terror erupts and can easily turn into conflict. When we feel insecure, we become anxious, angry, controlling, or withdrawn, often avoiding contact and staying distant. At the root of these emotions is the feeling that we are fighting for our lives. The need to feel secure is strong and primal. Experiencing an emotional and physical connection can soothe the pain of detachment. Blaming, shutting down, and stonewalling often characterize fights that follow disconnection. These behaviors are actually cries for help.

The fact is that we are emotionally attached to our partner and dependent upon them in much the same way that a child relies on a parent for nurturing, support, and protection. Our culture prizes independence and can hold *dependence* as a dirty word. But healthy adult attachment is essential in order for any partnership to thrive. When we don't have a reliable emotional connection in our most important relationships, we suffer. We might feel gloomy, angry, depressed or lonely. The intensity of these emotions is an essential part of the built-in survival mechanism that all human beings share. Without secure interpersonal bonds, we would perish, and some part of us knows it.

When we become aware of what we need in order to thrive, we begin by acting in ways that strengthen the quality our connection. A committed partnership can provide a container that holds a shared intention to fulfill our own and each other's need for security. When we can relax into the certainty of being securely attached, that ease not only permeates our relationship but enables it to become a safe haven from which we can venture out into the world of career, and meaningful purpose. Some would say that the fulfillment of this need is the most important thing we can pursue in this life. If it isn't, we don't know what is.

84.

Safety

Safety: "freedom from danger, risk, or injury"(*American Heritage Dictionary of the English Language*, 1969).

One complaint we often hear in our work with couples is "I don't feel safe." When we ask the speaker what he means, we get a variety of responses, such as "She blames me whenever there's a problem," or "He's always focused on what's wrong with me. He never has anything good to say about me," or "I feel like I'm always walking through a minefield. One false step and there will be an explosion," or "She never listens to me."

What it all boils down to is a fear that the other person may react to in ways that are painful. When we anticipate this kind of a reaction, we will likely be careful not to reveal anything that could put us at risk of being hurt. If the conversation does continue, the depth of the content will probably be superficial. There's nothing wrong with talking about the weather or sports, but if you want to have a more personal conversation, one in which there is a willingness to be vulnerable, it will not happen unless there is a feeling of mutual safety.

A safe space may be the most important element of a healthy relationship, and a failure to co-create it is one of the biggest factors in relationships that go flat, become distant, or become consumed by endless conflict. If one or both partners don't feel free to speak their true feelings without getting attacked, there is not an adequate amount of safety in the relationship. Until there is, the quality of connection will be unsatisfying to at least one of them—and in terms of relationships, if it's not working for one, it's not working! Many of us haven't had much exposure to relationships characterized by a high degree of emotional safety. It's hard to commit ourselves to something when we're not sure what it looks like or whether it's even a real possibility.

Creating a level of safety that is unconditionally, permanently secure and free from the possibility of getting our feelings hurt is impossible. We can do things to minimize the likelihood of emotionally injury, but getting hurt is a certainty. We are all humans who have good days and bad days, strengths and weaknesses. Even the most enlightened of us will on occasion let slip an unkind word from our lips that could cause a momentary "ouch." Fortunately, most of these blips can be quickly repaired, and often the relationship can be even stronger after the breakdown.

Perfectionistic expectations can be a setup for disappointment and resentment. When the inevitable glitches arise, we have an opportunity to apologize if we're the source of it. If we are the recipient of it, then we have the opportunity to practice forgiveness.

Here are some practices that can enhance feelings of safety:

- Take a pause of one or two breaths before you respond to an impulse to say something out of anger.
- Reflect on your intention as to what you want to have happen between you and your partner in your conversation.
- When you feel threatened, get vulnerable and express your feelings rather than becoming defensive.
- Ask more questions and make more requests.
- Keep in mind that most of us are easily hurt.
- Attune yourself to what the other person is feeling .
- Recognize your intention and express it to your partner.
- Reassure your partner that you mean well and want to be honest.
- Minimize or avoid lengthy explanations of why you feel the way you do and rationalizations that justify your feelings.

- Become a world-class listener.
- Seek to understand the other person's feelings.
- Remember that people don't care how much you know until they know how much you care.

The best we can do is the best we can do. But that doesn't mean that our best can't become better in the future with practice. Practice generally doesn't make perfect, but it does help. A lot. And fortunately, we all get lots of opportunities to practice.

85.

Ragers, bullies, and intimidators

Jonas and Patrice had been married for seven years, but things had been going downhill for the last three. Patrice felt increasingly frustrated over what she described as Jonas's refusal to accommodate her requests for more respectful responses to her concerns. She finally reached a point where she was unwilling to continue to tolerate his insults, and she announced that she was planning to leave the marriage. Upon hearing the news, Jonas flew into a rage and shouted, "You'll be sorry for this! I'm going to make you pay for breaking up our family."

Jonas refused to cooperate with the process to divide their assets and formalize their custody terms. Knowing that she was anxious to complete the divorce proceedings, he deliberately dragged the divorce out for over two years.

"I know that he did that just to torture me," Patrice said.

Whenever they had communication about the times to pick up and drop off the children, Jonas made hurtful remarks. He often indulged himself by speaking in derogatory ways to Patrice in front of the children. In an effort to remove herself from harm's way, Patrice asked her neighbor if she could bring the kids to her house to pick up and drop them off for their visit with their dad in order to avoid direct contact with him. The neighbor, who was well aware of Jonas's hot temper, willingly agreed.

When we last heard, Jonas still hadn't recovered from the divorce.

He didn't date or remarry, and he continued his vendetta for years. Although he genuinely loved his son and daughter and wanted to spend time with them, when they became teenagers, they refused to visit their dad. As adults, they have had only infrequent contact with him. Patrice was careful to not say anything negative about their dad, but Jonas was convinced that she had turned the children against him.

Jonas never did take any responsibility for the breakdown of his marriage, continuing to insist to anyone who would listen that it was all Patrice's fault and that she had planned the divorce from the beginning. He obsessed about his revenge fantasies, wishing harm to Patrice. He never realized that it was largely his own vindictiveness that took the marriage down. Patrice eventually found another partner and got married, this time more happily.

It can be hard to accept that words can be as destructive as actions. Even words we believe are spoken out of an intention to serve our partner can be hurtful. Those spoken with disrespect, and out of an intention to coerce someone to take a desired action, may contain an implicit threat. And threats, whether overt or covert, are inherently intimidating and therefore damaging to the relationship.

In retrospect, Patrice was able to see that by tolerating years of disrespect from Jonas, she had unknowingly "created the monster" by enabling him to continue his behavior without repercussions. Patrice's unwillingness to take a stand reinforced Jonas's belief that he could continue his abusiveness with impunity.

Standing up to a bully is difficult and can be physically and emotionally dangerous; when they feel threatened, their attacks can intensify. Yet the longer a bully's bad behavior is tolerated, the more intimidating they become. A continued willingness to tolerate their threats, insults, and abuse can subject us to even graver dangers.

Patrice eventually did find the courage, strength, and support to do what she knew she had to do, to save the only life that she could save. Sometimes, that's what it comes down to.

86.
Who's got the power?

Most of us would agree that it's a good idea to share power in a relationship rather than having one partner be the one who always wields it. We concur with the principle of sharing power, but actually integrating it into our relationship can be challenging. There are miles of uncharted territory between an idea and its ultimate manifestation. When it comes to the reality of having to subordinate our authority to another, we might feel apprehensive about doing so.

Power has its prices and its benefits. While power is about having influence over our life, it is also associated with a wide range of experiences that include freedom, security, control, protection, and love. Power also requires us to be responsible for the choices we make. If we've been in a relationship in which we've traded some of our power to our partner for the security that they provide or for the responsibility they are willing to take, we may have doubts about our ability to assume that responsibility. If we've been out of practice in the art of skillfully wielding power, there may be a learning curve. And it could be steep.

The balance of power usually isn't consistent across the board. It's not uncommon for each partner to have a higher level of authority and expertise in different domains, such as household maintenance, finances, childcare, yard upkeep, social activities, vacation planning, and shopping. Moving into a higher level of responsibility in a domain in which we are less experienced can feel intimidating, and despite our desire for greater power, we may experience reluctance to take that step. This ambivalence can be internal and will not necessarily be discussed in the relationship. We may not even be consciously aware of the inner conflict between these two parts of ourselves.

Our partner may have similar concerns about redistributing power. They may be exhausted from carrying an excessive amount of responsibility and looking forward to unloading some of it. They may also think that they are the only ones who can do it "right."

When an inner conflict is not addressed, it will become an interpersonal conflict in which one's ambivalence will get projected onto the other person and played out. When each person views the other person as being at fault in a breakdown, there is a good chance that the relationship will fall into a downward spiral. When one person initiates the examination of the existing power structure, they should be specific and honest about their concerns. They can explain why reconsidering the power balance in the relationship is important to them.

The process of sharing power involves negotiation, commitment and vision. Remembering our vision helps us stay on track of our desired outcome. Successful relationships have agreements regarding power that work for both partners. Like any other skill, becoming competent in the art of negotiating power is best cultivated through practice. The more time we spend dealing with our interpersonal differences and internal conflicts, the less fearful we become about engaging complex feelings. The more we resist having the uncomfortable conversations, the more fearful of them we become. In becoming more skilled in confronting differences with clarity and goodwill, our confidence increases, and our skill level grows. And that's a good thing!

87.

Agreements

Charlie: Allan and I were friends in college. One of the things I liked about him was his honesty. Unlike a lot of other people I knew back then, he was very direct. There was no pretense, or at least very little that I could see. He was a straight shooter. And honesty was also one of the things that I didn't like about him, at least when it involved a truth I didn't want to hear.

One day, we made an agreement to meet at his apartment before going to the YMCA to play handball. I showed up fifteen minutes late. Knowing that Allan had a thing about punctuality, I had my excuse prepared when I arrived. "Hi, Al, sorry I'm late. I lost track of the time." He looked at me with one of "those" looks.

"You know, Charlie," he said, "this is becoming a habit with you, and I've got to tell you, it's starting to get to me."

To use the jargon of those times, I freaked out. "For Christ sakes, Allan, give me a break. I told you I was sorry. Nobody's perfect. Don't be so uptight! Take it easy. You're late sometimes too!"

Unruffled, Allan paused and responded to my outburst. "Yeah, I know you apologized. And I know that nobody's perfect, even me. And I know that you said you're sorry. And I still feel upset and disappointed, and frustrated now and when we have an agreement and you don't honor it but instead you bring me an excuse. Look, Charlie, why do you think I even bother telling you how I feel when you show up late or don't honor your end of an agreement?"

Me: "I don't know. Because you're pissed off?"

Allan: "I might be pissed off, but that's not why I tell you."

Me: "Because you want to make me feel bad?"

Allan: "No. That's not it either."

Me (now becoming angrier): "I don't know! You tell me!"

Allan: "Because if I don't tell you, then I'll end up feeling used and disrespected. I'll feel angry at you, and the feelings will probably contaminate my attitude towards you, and I'll end up not wanting to hang out with you so much, and you'll probably feel it too, and the distance between us will grow, and neither of us will bring it up, and then our friendship will fade away and eventually end. And I don't want that to happen."

Me (after a long pause): "Wow! Is that what you think will happen if you just let it go without making a mountain out of a molehill? Why do you think all that's going to happen?"

Allan: "Because it has happened with other friends. It happened because I was trying to be cool and pretend that some things were no big deal when in fact they were. And after the last time when I found myself feeling like I no longer liked one of my friends and coming up with reasons why I felt the way I did, I decided that I was going to be more honest in the future with people, even if they thought that I was stupid."

Me: "So, you don't want to risk losing our friendship, and that's why you told me how you felt?"

Allan (sarcastically): "I guess you could say that."

Me (sheepishly): "Wow. Well . . . thanks."

Allan: "You're welcome."

The incident I have described occurred over fifty years ago, and it remains one of the most powerful and valuable learning experiences I've ever had in my life. Allan and I went on to become best friends. One year later, we both graduated from college. In the year following that, Allan got married. I was his best man. In the following year, Linda and I got married. Allan was my best man. Allan and I remained best friends until his death in 1996.

Many lessons came out of that single incident, but one of the biggest had to do with what is most important, whether that be a marriage, a friendship, or any other significant relationship. Holding our word as sacred does not mean that we will never slip. We all make mistakes, have lapses, and occasionally fall off the wagon. When we are fortunate enough to have a friend or a life partner who is honest enough to risk upsetting us by sharing a difficult truth, we are truly blessed. And if we share our appreciation with that person for their doing so, we honor that person, honor ourselves, and honor our relationship.

Some gifts can last a lifetime, depending on our ability to see their value. Another lesson I gained was a willingness to take the risk of sharing my feelings with others in ways that are sensitive and respectful to their capacity to receive them. The qualities this commitment has compelled me to cultivate are generosity, integrity, courage, and discernment. I'm still working on it, but I'm making headway. I may not ever get to "perfect," but that's okay because I'm living in a "perfection-free zone," and that's good enough for me!

88.

Grievances

Grievances. We all have them. They are often about those little and not-so-little annoyances another person has caused. Sometimes we can overlook them or just let go of our irritation. At other times, we may need to address them. When our attempts to clear the air fail, and we continue to feel upset, those feelings turn into a grievance.

Holding the belief that no one is perfect and being forgiving of others' imperfections are two very different things. The first is a theory, an abstraction that exists as a philosophy, and the second is an expression of how we actually feel. When our concept of reality is aligned with our inner experience, there is harmony within ourselves and in our relationship. Problems tend to arise when we attribute the symptoms of our misalignment to others and hold them responsible for our dis-ease, which can damage the relationship. An ongoing failure to come to terms with grievances inevitably diminishes feelings of goodwill.

The vast majority of couples who break up do not do so as a result of a dramatic incident of violence or betrayal; they succumb to a gradual diminishment of affection, which is often caused by withheld feelings of resentment. Feelings of guilt, anger, or shame may cause them to become defensive, justify their actions, and invalidate the other person's feelings. They may even launch into an attack. This behavior can activate a destructive cycle of blame and defensiveness that is very difficult to neutralize.

The desire to build a case of unresolved grievances can be strong. It provides us a means of avoiding guilt, which enables us to experience a sense of superiority. This perceived advantage is overshadowed by its cost, a growing sense of resentment towards our partner. Repairing the damage caused by focusing on "evidence" of shortcomings requires us both to accept our share of responsibility.

While the thought of opening up this conversation may feel like a daunting prospect, the actual reality can be very different. Breaking the habit of collecting grievances and learning to respectfully express feelings before they become toxic can mean the difference between feeling cursed or feeling blessed. Once we get into the habit of being intolerant of unfinished business, we'll never want to go back to the old way.

89.

What we appreciate appreciates.

The word *appreciate* has two meanings. The first definition refers to the admiration or assignment of value to someone or something, as in "I appreciate your willingness to be honest with me," or "I appreciate how much time you put into completing this project." The second definition has to do with an increase in value, such as with a home, a vintage wine, or a friendship. Gratitude is the experience of acknowledging our appreciation for what we have.

When cultivating the attitude of gratitude, we focus our attention on what we have rather than what we lack. In the process, it becomes possible to cultivate an appreciation of the ordinary, particularly those aspects of life that we may have previously taken for granted. This attitude is one in which saying "Thank you" springs forth naturally rather than in an obligatory way. When we live in an ongoing state of gratitude, we re-sensitize ourselves to the beauty of small things. Gratitude is a living ritual, and like prayer, it can be practiced whenever the feeling spontaneously arises or at designated times. There are some common times to practice, like when waking up in the morning, before bedtime, and before a meal. It is the depth of the connection to what we are feeling at the time that impacts our experience. The more specific we are about what we are grateful for, the greater the benefit.

Resistance to change can take many forms, such as a tendency to complain—to be in a mood of grievance and self-pity. Gratitude is the antidote to feeling that we don't have enough: enough love, money, time, friends, security, or whatever we believe to be missing in our life. We have worked with people who are so rich that they literally don't know what to do with their money. Yet they constantly worry that they don't have enough wealth and are obsessed with the idea that they need to accumulate more. Although this perceived deficiency is not grounded in reality, for them the need feels real. They have spent so much time focusing on their desire for more wealth that they become habituated to seeing the world through the lens of insufficiency. Consequentially, they never feel satiated.

This feeling of insufficiency can spread into other areas of our life, including our relationships. We will likely view our partner in terms of what they are not providing for us rather than what they are. This attitude often causes us to view our partner with judgment, criticism, or even contempt for failing to make us happy. When we view our partner through these negative filters, they can't help but feel our judgments, whether we speak them aloud or not. They in turn feel unappreciated and unloved and may be disinclined to want to give love to us, reaffirming our feeling that we are not receiving the love we want and deserve. This vicious circle, if uninterrupted, will produce catastrophic results.

The antidote to freeing ourselves from this cycle, or to avoiding it altogether, is to recognize that the source of our disappointment may have more to do with our own attitude than it does with our partner's failings. We may both be disregarding the part we each are playing in the situation and projecting all of the blame onto the other. When we finally see our part in things, we are less likely to hold the other person responsible for the circumstance in which we find ourselves. Consequently, they feel less blamed and shamed and more open to listening and responding nondefensively.

The invocation of an attitude of gratitude is simple but not necessarily easy, primarily because it can feel very vulnerable to accept our part in a relationship breakdown, particularly when we've spent a lot of time reaffirming our innocence and our partner's guilt. But the good news is that although it isn't easy, it is possible. And when both people are doing their own work together, the shift can occur very quickly. Yet even when only one person is doing the work, things can change. In most cases, the other person often joins them. In those situations where the other person refuses to stop blaming and feeling victimized even after a long period of time, there may be a need for professional help.

It is possible to make a conscious choice to focus on what we really like about other people, and our life in general. This practice of intentionally viewing others through the eyes of appreciation can become a habit that expresses itself effortlessly. Acknowledgments freely given without coercion are appreciation in its purest form. And that is one of the sweetest things we can give to our partner, to ourselves, and to all of our relationships!

90.
Complaints are highly underrated.

Complaint: "an expression of dissatisfaction or annoyance about a
state of affairs; a statement that a situation is unsatisfactory
or unacceptable"

The American Heritage Dictionary of the English Language, 1969

Charlie: Nobody likes a complainer. At least, as a kid that's the message I got either literally or implicitly from most of the adults in my life whenever I expressed my dissatisfaction with things like certain rules, demands, or other conditions I was expected to accommodate. I wasn't being rebellious (well, maybe sometimes I was); I was simply expressing my perspective and my sincere desire to understand something I couldn't comprehend. It wasn't that I wanted to know why these standards were in place and where they came from. I wanted to know who had the authority to authorize this agreement about why things had to be this way. And how do they know?

I was one of those irritating kids who was always asking, "Why?"

"Why do we have to pledge allegiance to the flag every day?"

"Why do people intentionally try to hurt other people?"

"Why do you and Mom fight so much?"

"Why do I have to go to college?"

"Why do I have to wait until I'm sixteen in order to get my driver's license?"

And "If God is loving and compassionate, why does he allow so much suffering in the world?"

My questions ran the gamut from relatively trivial and personal concerns to profound philosophical issues. I was still in grade school when I stopped asking my questions—because I never received answers.

One way to avoid responding to someone's grievance is to make them wrong for expressing their concern and invalidate the legitimacy of their complaint.

The problem with having a policy of avoidance is that when there is a refusal to address complaints, the underlying concerns do not go away. When suppressed, they grow stronger. Over time they become increasingly toxic, contaminating the quality of the relationship itself. This amplifies the grievance and can lead to a breakdown in interpersonal trust, the intentional or unconscious sabotage of commitments, passive-aggressive behaviors, deep-seated resentments, and a host of other relationship problems.

There is such a thing as making a responsible complaint—one in which the complainer isn't simply expressing their unhappiness with the expectation that "somebody needs to do something about it." Responsible complaints include the complainer's commitment to be a part of the solution.

Yet even in situations in which a complaint is expressed in a nonresponsible way, there can still be value in considering the complainer's grievance. Regardless of how they express their concern, if it is not met with at least some degree of consideration, the dissatisfaction will likely go underground and manifest itself at some point.

For those considering the question of whether or how to express a complaint, keep in mind that the way it is expressed is one of the main factors determining the kind of response that will be forthcoming. Registering responsible complaints does not make one a whiner or a victim but rather someone who cares about the system within which they are operating—whether that be a place of employment, a marriage, or a friendship—and is willing to risk ruffling a few feathers in order to bring about potentially positive systemic changes and to prevent negative ones.

Complaints can be the first step in opening the door to the

remediation of conditions that require attention; they can illuminate what we don't want and what isn't working for us. If a relationship isn't working for both parties, it isn't working. Complaints provide important information regarding if and where the system needs adjustment. The sooner we act on this information, the sooner necessary corrections can be implemented.

It's no accident that the most successful relationships and organizations view the expression of responsible feedback as critical to the health of the system. The old saying "No news is good news" does not apply when it comes to unexpressed grievances. And neither does the saying "If you don't have something nice to say, don't say anything at all." It's possible that not everything our parent(s) told us is true. But don't tell them we told you that!

91.

When being wrong is all right

When it comes to relationships, the ten most powerful words you might ever hear are "You can be right, or you can have a relationship." And the most powerful word of those ten is *or*. We can have either one or the other, but we can't have both. Our friend Amy shared a great "being right" story with us that was life changing. Early in her marriage, Amy and her husband, Phillip, traveled to England to visit his side of the family. Phillip's mom planned a big dinner party—roasting chickens and inviting aunts, uncles, and cousins—in honor of the couple. On the day before the festivities, Phillip's brother offered to take care of their two-year-old daughter so that Amy and Phillip could spend a romantic evening alone together. When Amy's mother-in-law, Diane, heard that they had gone out to dinner without inviting her to join them, she became enraged.

While Diane could be difficult, her response was over the top and extreme, even for her. She ranted and raved over the telephone, calling Amy selfish and inconsiderate for not inviting her to join them. She concluded her tirade by announcing that she had canceled the dinner celebration and thrown all the food into the garbage.

Amy was shocked by the whole episode. She felt misunderstood, hurt, and violated by the attack. Part of her wanted to tell her mother in law to "shove it" and get on the next plane to the USA, and another part felt saddened and deeply disappointed in her lost opportunity to create a favorable impression with Phillip's family. She was caught between two powerful impulses. Phillip was supportive and told Amy, "I don't think you did anything wrong. It's my mother that is way out of line here. I wouldn't blame you if you never wanted anything to do with her again. If that's your choice, I support it."

Amy was so relieved to feel understood and validated by her husband that she calmed down and began to think the situation through. A short time later, she came back to Phillip and said, "You only have one mother. It's not acceptable for me to separate myself from her. It's just not right."

Then she called her mother-in-law and apologized to her, saying, "It was inconsiderate of me to go out to dinner with Phillip and not invite you to come along. We don't see you often enough, and I want to spend time with you when we come to visit. I hope you can forgive me and come to dinner with us tonight." Diane accepted her apology, and they repaired their damaged relationship.

Not long after this incident, Amy's mother-in-law came down with a mysterious illness. She was not properly diagnosed at first, but later it was determined that she had AIDS. In the early stages of her illness, Phillip and Amy learned that one complication of AIDS can be dementia and that the incident in England had been the first in a series of irrational outbursts resulting from the illness's impact on her brain functioning.

Shortly after the diagnosis, Diane moved in with Amy and Phillip, and Amy became her primary caregiver until the time of her death. Caring for her mother-in-law proved to be one of the most fulfilling experiences of Amy's life and of Diane's as well. These two women who both shared a deep love for the same man created a depth of connection with each other that neither of them could have previously imagined possible. Even though Amy was young at the time, she was wise and generous of spirit. In taking responsibility for the breakdown, she set her mother-in-law's mind and heart at ease. Amy didn't simply stuff her hurt and anger; she let it go so that she could be genuinely warm with her mother-in-law.

We are all challenged at times to become bigger than who we consider ourselves to be—more generous, more forgiving, more responsible, more courageous, more understanding, and more compassionate. When people hurt or frighten us and the differences between us erupt in anger, we have an opportunity to practice and strengthen these qualities.

Accepting the reality that being right is not an "and" but an "or" when it comes to relationships can help us make the choice that supports our highest priority. When we experience the richness of a loving connection, not being right seems like a small price to pay for all the benefits that connection provides. Life offers us countless opportunities to practice letting go of self-righteousness, probably more than we want. Doing so allows us to fulfill our universal longing for connection. In terms of the outcome, being right loses every time!

92.

Damage control

If you've ever been in the middle of a painful breakdown with someone and felt overwhelmed with rage, fear, pain, despair, or some combination of the above, you're not alone. Even couples who have great relationships can occasionally experience feelings like this. It can seem like turning this situation into a learning opportunity just isn't going to happen, and the best that you can hope for is to do enough damage control to prevent things from falling into the "catastrophic" category. And even doing that, at times, is no small feat.

Try as we may to avoid doing or saying things that could cause upsets, sometimes things get worse before they get better. At this point the challenge is to bring more goodwill to our dialogue by seeing and relating to the other person as a partner rather than as an adversary. After all, it's likely that we both want the same result: an outcome that satisfies both of our needs and desires and does not diminish the quality of our relationship. We just have different strategies about how to get there.

This may at times seem like an impossible goal, but when we can agree to the desired outcome, the difference in our perspectives about how to achieve it can seem more resolvable. This usually involves a willingness for each partner to consider taking small steps towards the other person's concerns. It also requires one to take the first step, even though we might prefer that to be the other one. Also, slowing down the rhythm of the interaction and lowering the volume can help to bring about a more receptive and calmer quality of communication that can at the very least keep the level of antagonism from rising still higher.

Until we are able to resist the temptation to indulge ourselves with defensive or aggressive reactions in the face of provocation, our responses to conflict will probably just add fuel to the fire. The process of creating a successful partnership tends to be incremental rather than instantaneous. Relationship building can feel like we're standing near a very hot fire. And then there are times when we feel that we are standing *in* the fire. When we hold our goal as the fulfillment of both partners' needs rather than the satisfaction of our own desires, there is a shift not only in the outcome of our interaction but in the quality of our relationship. It is no longer based upon zero-sum thinking where there are winners and losers but becomes about defining "winning" as a function of mutual satisfaction. And if you think that such thinking is Pollyanna-ish and unrealistic in the "real world," think again. Or better still, try it out and see for yourself whether this is a fantasy or a genuine possibility!

93.
Thinking about getting marriage counseling?

"Marriage is a pit full of pitfalls devised by a devious deity for our conscious evolution."

—Wavy Gravy

Very few couples who have been together for a while have managed to avoid the pitfalls that often occur in committed partnerships. We know (personally and professionally) many couples who were convinced that their relationship was the exception to this rule and found after the first major disappointment, or the first child, or the first serious disagreement, or the last straw, that they were wrong. And while some couples do experience deep marital fulfillment with little serious conflict along the way, for the vast majority of couples, stuff happens.

Noted marriage researcher John Gottman claims that the average couple entering marriage counseling has been in a troubled relationship for over six years. That could be one of the reasons marriage counseling has gotten a lot of bad press and has the lowest satisfaction rating of all the different types of psychotherapy. As with a cancer diagnosis, early detection and treatment is a big plus.

While past generations of couples have taken the attitude of "grin and bear it" when difficulties arise in their relationship, these days most couples are unwilling to tolerate an unhappy marriage for very long without making an effort to repair broken places with books, DVDs, workshops, or couples' retreats. If none of these resources prove sufficiently helpful, there is, finally, the option of marriage counseling. If you are ever in a position in which you are considering that possibility, there are a few things you might want to consider before (and after) you make that decision.

It's not necessary to wait until both partners are completely on board with the idea of getting professional help. If one person is clear that they feel the need for another set of eyes and ears, it's probably time. One way to minimize potential conflict around this decision is to make an agreement that either partner has the authority to unilaterally exercise the couples' therapy option if they feel it's necessary. The best time to create this agreement is before rather than after the relationship has begun to deteriorate.

There are some important factors to keep in mind:

- Timing is everything. The question of when you choose to go is an important one. Waiting too long can be very costly, in more ways than one. The more entrenched the problems, the longer it takes to resolve them. By all means, make your best effort to repair your relationship, but if those efforts are not fruitful, it may be time to get help.
- Choose a person you both feel you can work with. There is no generic answer to the question of how you can be certain you have the right counselor, but it is important to both be in agreement that this is someone with whom you can at least begin the process.
- Beware of therapists who require you to commit to a fixed number of sessions before you've gotten to know their work.
- Be willing to ask your counselor any questions you feel might be relevant to your ability to accurately assess their competence and fit for you, such as their experience, credentials, success rate, education, or even marital status and history. If the counselor refuses to answer or turns your request into a question, you might want to think about seeking help elsewhere.
- Get clear about what you really want to get out of the counseling process. Couples come into counseling with a wide range of intentions, some conscious and some unconscious. Some

just seek to deal with the situation that brought them there and get back to their "normal level of relatedness." Others may be looking for a transcendent experience, of spiritual enlightenment.

- Your counselor is a consultant, not a fixer. Although couples may strongly disagree on many points, one thing they often agree on is that it is the therapist's responsibility to fix the marriage. After all, why else pay them all that money? The truth, however, is that couples therapy requires both partners to be active agents in the healing process rather than passive recipients to the service provider.

- The marriage counselor is there to assist and guide you to consider new patterns of behavior and new ways of looking at things—to redirect the focus of your attention away from your partner's behavior and more towards yourself.

- Your therapist might offer you tools or suggestions in order to change the dynamics of your relationship. Your job is to be as honest and engaged as you can be and to explore new possibilities.

- The real "work" of relationship counseling occurs between sessions. The counselor's office is the place where many of the lessons are learned, but knowing what you need to do generally isn't enough to bring about real change. Real change requires you to engage practices in your daily life that will enhance the development of the qualities you seek to strengthen.

It's in our life outside of the office where we get to practice and ultimately integrate new styles of relating and communicating that invite openness and trust and discourage avoidance and defensiveness. If you feel that it's easier to implement those changes in the therapy office than it is at home, that's probably because your counselor's added support has created a safety net enabling you to risk more emotional vulnerability.

Knowing when you need outside help and seeking it isn't a sign of weakness; it's a sign of intelligence. Almost every one of the couples whom we interviewed for our second book, *The Secrets of Great Marriages*, at one time or another received help to manage challenges that had arisen that required outside support. Help is available, not just in the form of counseling but through the wisdom, support, and shared life experiences of others who have walked this path and learned valuable lessons. Given what's at stake, we can all use all the help we can get!

94.

Constructive criticism generally isn't constructive.

Criticize: "to judge with severity, to find fault with, censure; usually implying a detailed expression of disapproval"

The American Heritage Dictionary of the English Language, 1969

Fault, severity, censure, disapproval—is it any wonder that we often cringe when someone asks if it's okay to give us some "constructive criticism"? It's actually a trick question, since that someone is probably aware that (1) we are not really interested in hearing their criticism, since if we were, we would have asked them for it, and (2) it's hard to tell them that it's not okay, since that would make us seem closed to their opinion.

If we do want to hear some constructive criticism, there's no problem. We shouldn't be surprised if we feel defensive or have the desire to justify after we've heard their comments. We can't really know in advance whether we will find their criticism helpful, but the odds are that this person has some other agenda they hope to fulfill.

For example, since it feels good to help someone who is struggling with a challenge, they may want us to accept their offer in order to feel helpful. Or they may want to demonstrate their intelligence in order to make a favorable impression on us. Or they may see their own value as being dependent upon their ability to help others be happier or more successful. Or they may want to help us because they care about us. Nothing wrong with that.

However, most criticism, constructive or otherwise, contains an implicit hope that we will approve of what they are offering and act accordingly. If we get defensive—that is, try to explain why we're not ready to do that right now, or justify why their advice doesn't work for us—they may feel offended or disappointed.

It's natural to become defensive if we feel judged by another's responses to what we've said or done. The challenge in situations like this is to honor our own feelings without disrespecting the other person. It's possible to accept, not necessarily agree with, their response, and to resist the temptation to explain ourselves, since it could cause them to feel judged and then get defensive.

It's helpful to remember that, almost always, at least a part of the other person's motivation comes from a worthy intention. The objective is to listen to their response, criticism and all, without getting defensive. Simply saying something like "Thanks," or "That gives me something to think about," or "I appreciate what you said," acknowledges that you've heard their words without either agreeing or disagreeing with them. If they press you and want to know whether you agree, just be honest and say that you need to think about it before you decide whether or not you plan to act on their advice. Also, see if you can find at least one thing in what they said that you liked, learned from, or agreed with, and tell them.

Everything we've written here about how to deal with those who want to give us constructive criticism applies to those of us on the other side, with a strong urge to tell someone else what we think they need to do, say, feel, think, or be. The next time the shoe is on the other foot, and we're the one asking if we can offer constructive criticism, we can give ourselves a quick time-out, to check our intention in giving it. When we think before we speak, it just might save us a lot of trouble. But of course, that's just my opinion.

95.
Sarcasm: sometimes it's not so funny.

C harlie: I grew up in a family in which communication and entertainment frequently involved the use of humor. I learned to use language to make puns and plays on words that earned me points in the eyes of my parents, both of whom were skilled in the language arts. One of my family's most frequently utilized forms of humor was sarcasm, so I came to see it as a normal means of self-expression.

Consequently, I learned to recognize opportunities to insert my sarcastic (characterized by my parents as "witty") responses to demonstrate my cleverness and got to enjoy the literal and verbal applause that often came from my words. When I was on the receiving end of sarcasm, however, I often felt a vague or at times acute sense of discomfort as though I were the butt of someone's joke. Because we viewed sarcasm as normal and even good since it provided amusement to everyone, I assumed that I was just overly sensitive and taking a playful discourse too seriously.

It wasn't until I left home that I became aware that not everyone uses or appreciates sarcasm. I discovered that many people, particularly those who grew up in homes that were sarcasm-free, were often hurt or offended by what felt to them like shaming judgments. One day, my friend Karl told me that he didn't appreciate a sarcastic remark that I had made and told me that I used sarcasm a lot. My response was to immediately get defensive, to make him wrong for being so thin skinned and unable to take a joke.

To his credit, Karl stuck to his guns and asked me to be less liberal with my sarcastic remarks. I felt somewhat less defensive after our talk but still upset—not just because of what felt like Karl's criticism of me but also because I felt bad for causing him to feel hurt.

Even though this conversation took place over forty years ago, it is still vivid in my memory. Today I feel deeply grateful to Karl for having had the courage to let a friend know that something he had done or said had been hurtful. Karl raised my awareness of the shadow side of sarcasm, which enabled me to see that not everyone appreciates it or sees sarcasm as a playful form of banter.

My consciousness was raised and has stayed that way over the years. And while to this day I sometimes find myself using sarcasm, particularly when I'm in a conversation where others are doing so, I'm less inclined to use it. The word *sarcasm* comes from the Greek word *sarkasmos*, which means "the tearing of flesh." It's no wonder that sarcasm often has a biting quality! While most sarcasm users would vehemently deny that they have any intention to cause pain to another person, sarcasm can be an indirect expression of unconscious resentment. This is not always the case, but it behooves us to be mindful of any tendency we might have to use sarcasm and to realize that it's not just sticks and stones that can be painful; words also can be.

Breaking the habit of sarcasm is not easy, particularly when we have been reinforcing it for many years. But when we see and feel the results of this practice, it's much harder to continue to indulge that habit. Going on a sarcasm fast may be one of the best things we can do for our relationships. Take it from one who knows that territory!

96.
Creative synthesis

In 2007, we attended a conference in Dubrovnik, Croatia, in which many other speakers from a number of countries shared stories about peacemaking between groups, individuals, and nations. One of these speakers was Johan Galtung. Galtung, who is a Norwegian sociologist and founder of the Peace Research Institute in Oslo, is a world-renowned expert in conflict resolution. Although he was over eighty at the time, he was one of the most dynamic speakers of the conference.

We were fortunate to spend time speaking with him after the conference and during a trip he made to San Francisco a couple of years later. In his talk, Galtung referred to a consultation he'd had years earlier when he was asked to mediate a border dispute between the countries of Ecuador and Peru. As in many places, the border was a body of water. In this case, however, the river between them appeared and disappeared according to temperature and rainfall. The area in dispute was a zone of 500 kilometers, and for the past fifty-four years, there had been endless "negotiations" (which were really verbal warfare), postponement, avoidance, and three bloody wars.

Each country was stuck in a mindset that the zone in dispute was owned by them alone, and the other country would have to give in. After over half a century, both sides were tired of fighting but were at a loss for how to resolve things. A suggestion was made to call in Galtung. After being briefed on the situation, Galtung offered something radical. He proposed that both countries assume joint ownership of the disputed area and draw no border at all. They would declare it a binational zone, consisting of a natural park for camping, hiking, and mountain climbing, and charge admission to those using the area, with both countries sharing in the proceeds. In 1998, a peace treaty between Ecuador and Peru officially designated the area as a natural park, a potent example of conflict transformation based on creativity and goodwill. Galtung referred to the conflict resolution process as "creative synthesis"—which he described as "the combination of smaller constituent elements forming a more complex whole and the driving force of modern creation, innovation, and intelligence."

Unlike many other programs designed to resolve differences between parties, creative synthesis does not involve a compromise where both parties end up feeling that they have given up too much. The breakthrough occurs when each party commits itself to transcend their old way of either/or thinking. In this example, the dialogue continued even in the face of frustration where both parties stayed engaged. While breaks and time-outs may be needed, there is an arrangement to return to the table until a mutual agreement that satisfies the needs of both parties is in place.

Not surprisingly, creative synthesis works for couples as well as nations. Creativity is an essential quality in any breakdown where one or both parties are unable to fulfill their needs. When there is a shared commitment to resolve the impasse in a way that results in mutual satisfaction, there is a likelihood not only that resolution will occur but also that it will be lasting.

When we practice conscious combat as opposed to fighting, the struggle tends to become more creative and is more likely to result in growth and development. There is so much at stake. The desire to get our way vies for dominance with the part that seeks harmony and cooperation.

The process takes into consideration the goals of both personal gain *and* mutual satisfaction. This dialogue is characterized by a spirit of goodwill, which ultimately enables both partners to feel heard and understood. Rather than holding an intention for victory at any cost, the ultimate goal is to remain in dialogue until a mutually acceptable solution is found.

If the Peruvian and Ecuadorian negotiators were able to prevent a war with creative synthesis, the rest of us should have a (non) fighting chance!

97.

Are you a champion of repair?

"Evolution is an error-making and an error-correcting process."

Jonas Salk MD

We're all mistake-prone, to varying degrees. No one is perfect, and while it is a worthwhile intent to minimize the frequency of our mistakes, it's a good idea to put some time into becoming more competent in our ability to correct the mistakes we will inevitably make on the path of relationship.

One very common mistake is to argue in defense of our own innocence, usually in an effort to divert blame and responsibility onto another. Unfortunately, freeing ourselves from ingrained defensive habits can be difficult when we've been exercising them for years or even decades. It takes time as well as many repetitions to override old behavior patterns and install new ones. It's likely that at least at first, we won't be able to prevent or even interrupt all of our unhealthy impulses. So, for those times that we fail to block the impulse to get defensive or offensive, here are some things that help to repair damage:

- Acknowledge what you've just done or said. The sooner you do so, the better. Doing so will likely provide your partner, who may be feeling hurt or angry, enough comfort to diminish the intensity of their feelings. This will enable you both to engage in a more rational, less emotionally charged dialogue.
- Although it *does* take two to tango, it only takes one to invite the other person to the dance. The best way to issue an invitation

to the dance of repair is for one person (it doesn't matter which one) to acknowledge that a breakdown has occurred, to accept responsibility for their contribution to it, and to express an intention to repair whatever hard feelings may have been activated. It's important that the person who takes this first step not demand that the other do the same and acknowledge their part in the breakdown. Hopefully they will, without your encouragement, but even if they don't, it's best not to insist.

- Another element in the repair process has to do with apologizing. If you feel some remorse over anything you might have done or said and can issue an honest apology, you should go ahead and do so, but only if it's truly sincere. Sincerity means that you are expressing your apology out of a genuine feeling of remorse and from a desire to restore more trust and goodwill back into the relationship. If your apology is coming from a desire to appease or placate your partner, she will likely sense that your motivation is insincere and will probably not be particularly appreciative of it.

- In cases where you experience yourself to have been offended or disrespected, the challenge is to express your feelings without assassinating your partner's character and without an intention to punish them for their actions or words. Since it is natural to experience these impulses, using self-restraint at these times can be difficult but not impossible. Try to resist the temptation to go for the jugular in response to what you have just received. It's usually best to allow unkind words to go without counterattacking. If your partner apologizes or acknowledges their role in the breakdown, forgiveness can go a long way, but only if you feel ready to forgive them.

- When you express your feelings and concerns, focus on your partner's words and/or actions that were hurtful or offensive to you rather than on them personally. When referring to the interaction that was upsetting to you, speak of what your partner actually did or said rather than what kind of a person you see them as being. Don't call them names or project negative characterizations. Instead, specifically identify what you experienced in response to their reaction, such as "When you walked away from me in the middle of my sentence, I felt disrespected and I was furious at you." Or "When you mentioned divorce, I felt frightened and I just shut down."

- Speaking from personal experience rather than being accusatory will support the repair process and help to restore trust. It's easy to underestimate how sensitive most of us are to feeling threatened or blamed. One thing that will make a big difference in your ability to make successful repairs when they are needed is to minimize your use of the word *you*, which is likely to activate defensiveness on their part. Replacing it when you can with "we," as in "We have a problem that I am committed to having us solve," can do a lot to keep the channels of listening and receptivity open.

- It's always a good idea to listen without interrupting your partner when they are speaking, even if they are saying something you believe to be inaccurate. Interruptions rarely clarify things or improve the climate of trust and respect during an interaction. If you have an issue with something your partner says, make a mental note of it and bring it up after they have completed what they want to say. If they interrupt you, let them know that you need a little more time to complete what you have to say and respectfully request that they hold their concerns until after you're done, as you are trying to do with them.

- Keep in mind that even those couples with the best relationships have their moments. What distinguishes them from couples whose relationships are not the best is their ability to recognize when a repair is called for and their willingness to promptly and skillfully initiate the repair process.

These are a few of the things to remember when we hold an intention to repair a damaged relationship. If your best efforts don't do the trick, it's time to bring in some support. But only after you've given it your best shot!

98.

Clearing

When strong emotions get activated within us, as they inevitably do in close relationships, it can seem as though we have only two options: to vent our feelings outwardly or stuff them. Stuffing is a form of withholding and denial to both ourselves and to the other person. There is a third option that appears to be the same as stuffing but is distinct from it in an important way. It's referred to as "clearing."

When we experience unpleasant feelings, our initial impulse is to try to eradicate them in order to bring us back a less troubled frame of mind. It's not always necessary to communicate all of our feelings, but some emotional responses can't be cleared without expressing them.

The clearing process involves taking a moment to reflect upon whether the response we're having to the other person's words or actions is something we can let go of without feeling incomplete. Stuffing feelings impacts our relationship and our inner experience. Those emotions don't disappear when we've put them in the denial zone. It's a good idea to relinquish distressing feelings if it can be done in a way that really does neutralize our emotional state. It's critically important that we're honest with ourselves as to whether we have actually cleared our feelings or have merely stuffed them. Sometimes it's hard to tell. When we have cleared our feelings, we're no longer preoccupied with residual thoughts or emotions; they have been neutralized. If, however, we find ourselves obsessed with concerns related to the incident, we may need to speak with the person with whom we feel unfinished.

Since many of us prefer not to have a direct encounter with someone with whom there is an incompletion, we may be predisposed to see things as finished when they are not in order to avoid an uncomfortable conversation. It may become apparent in the minutes, hours, or days following an incident that we need to have the "we need to talk" conversation after all. Clearing, whether it's done internally or interpersonally, needs to happen sooner or later. And although sooner is always better than later, it's never too late to acknowledge what we weren't in touch with at the time it occurred.

Making our intention clear in bringing up our concern can set a context for a productive conversation. Bringing a positive intention in an effort to create completion in a relationship will reassure our partner that we mean well and that we have a sense of hopefulness.

An incompletion is anything we feel needs to be said. It can be an expression of regret ("I wish that I had thanked you for the gift you gave me the other day"). It can be the expression of a reaction to a perceived insult ("My feelings were hurt when you didn't introduce me to your boss at the party last night") or of a grievance ("This is the second time this week that you showed up late for an appointment that we had, and I want to let you know that I'm disappointed").

Sharing disappointment can activate defensive responses, but when we don't clear unresolved feelings, they will continue to diminish the level of mutual trust and respect. Also, the chances of the disappointing actions continuing will be increased if the other person is not made aware of how their behavior has affected us.

Not all disappointments need to be addressed interpersonally. Some can be relinquished without even bringing our feelings to the other person's attention, if they are simply minor irritants. Disappointments only become incomplete when our best efforts to clear them within ourselves fail to get the job done.

Clearing has another valuable effect. During the times when we cannot remove the feelings completely, we may at least be able to settle them down so that by the time we bring them up in conversation, instead of coming out with a blaming tone or a combative posture, we do so in a way that invites understanding.

Regardless of how we deal with the breakdowns, letdowns, and bring downs that occur, the bottom line has to do with maintaining the integrity of the relationship, free of any obstructions that can send us off course. Incompletions are like dirty dishes in the sink. They don't go away or clean themselves if left unattended; they only get dirtier and harder to clean. And incompletions occur in every relationship. The question is if and how we deal with them when they do.

99.

When he (or she) won't open up

A frequent complaint we hear from our clients and students (and admittedly, it tends to be women who are voicing it) is that one partner is resistant to talking. This complaint is often followed by statements like "I can't get him to open up. No matter what I do, I get nothing more than a one-word response. Sometimes I don't even get that!"

No one likes to hear bad news, but sometimes refusing to talk about upsetting issues can be far more damaging than discussing them. If one partner refuses to participate in a conversation, either directly or by being unavailable, this creates a vicious cycle of alienation or even contempt. The resistant partner may be overt or covert about closing down lines of communication. Direct refusals to engage like "I don't want to talk about it" often contain an implicit threat. It's a warning that they will leave or punish the other person. Such exchanges can turn into a contest of wills where one partner is communicating that they won't "give in" to the other person's desire to talk.

The resistant partner needs to know that becoming less defensive doesn't necessarily translate into submitting to another person's will. But it requires the ability to see beyond the either/or thinking that such impasses can create. The partner who shuts down may appear angry, but other feelings are likely at play. It's likely that they are fearful too. Frequently, the partner who doesn't want to talk is afraid that they won't be able to hold their ground. They may feel less skilled at articulating their concerns. The initiator, on the other hand, may be motivated by fear that if a purposeful conversation doesn't occur, the relationship will be jeopardized. This is a common scenario. It's not unusual for one person to be more concerned about the stability of the relationship and the other to be more acutely sensitive to a loss of freedom.

Both connection and personal autonomy are essential aspects of any committed partnership. When the relationship bond is threatened, the partner who is more attuned to connection has a stronger motivation to fix what they perceive as an imbalance in the system. In all likelihood, their efforts to create engagement will be met with a less-than-enthusiastic response. The challenge here is for the initiator to resist the temptation to throw their hands up in exasperation. One way to approach the issue is to say, "We've got a problem," a nonaccusatory way of expressing concern.

Until both partners share a more equal level of concern about their connection, responsibility for addressing the issue will fall to the more motivated partner. What does not work is to become resigned to tolerating a distant, cold relationship, which is a prescription for misery.

Here are a few guidelines to help to break the impasse:

- Create an agreement to discuss the issue. If now isn't a good time, find a time that works for you both and commit to it. When you do sit down to talk, both of you state your intentions for what you'd like to have happen. For example, "I hope that we can both feel closer."
- Be proactive. Approach the conversation with an intention to not only listen to what your partner is saying but to understand their feelings.
- Take responsibility. Keep in mind that in all breakdowns, both partners have played a part in creating the problematic circumstances. Accepting this responsibility empowers each of you to interrupt the cycle of blame.
- Remember that it's possible to interrupt deeply embedded patterns even when there has been a history of previous failures. Hold a vision of success.

- Speak in ways that promote trust, respect, safety, and vulnerability.
- Resist the temptation to justify your position.
- At first seek to understand rather than to be understood. The time for being understood will come after your partner feels heard.
- Be patient. These situations usually don't resolve themselves in a single conversation.
- Acknowledge incremental improvements and express appreciation for them.
- At the end of the conversation, thank your partner for their participation, regardless of the outcome of the dialogue, and if necessary, voice a desire to continue the conversation at a later date.

Taking these steps can move a painful breakdown into a transformative breakthrough. Sometimes a little correction can go a very long way.

100.

It's never too late to have a happy childhood. —Tom Robbins

T he term *unfinished business*—or what we refer to as "incompletions"—in the context of relationships refers to any experiences or communications that we have shared together that have left one or both of us feeling unresolved. It usually involves a feeling that something remains unsaid, leaving us feeling unsettled, with a sense that we're not done yet. Many of us have unfinished business from the distant past that continues to impact current relationships. Unfinished business can go as far back as early childhood and cause us to relate to the person in our current relationship as though they were the same one who distressed us years ago. This "mistaken identity" or "transference" can, predictably, create present-day relationship problems.

We often feel unfinished because we haven't sufficiently attended to feelings evoked from past interactions. Inadequately processed emotions can easily get transferred to current situations, causing distress in both partners. At these times, what is called for is a degree of trust shared by both partners that was not experienced at the time of the original breakdown. One factor that will enhance the feelings of safety is the commitment to the process of becoming complete. Commitment provides security that our partner won't leave or punish us if we say disturbing things. When we feel this way, we are more inclined to allow unexpressed feelings to rise into our awareness and permit ourselves to communicate them.

When we become close to each other, incomplete issues reveal themselves and can cause discomfort, which can motivate us to recognize the link between our past experiences and our present circumstances. In this self-reflection we are likely to become more aware of previous experiences that activated similar feelings that felt threatening to us. When we turn towards rather than away from painful feelings from the past, healing becomes available. At this point we begin engaging in self-reflective questions:

- Which of my needs have I been neglecting or ignoring?
- Which needs am I holding my partner responsible for fulfilling?
- What risks am I willing to take in order to feel more self-accepting?
- What do I fear in being more assertive?
- What do I fear in being more vulnerable and accommodating to my partner?

When we begin to address these and other questions, old patterns that may have been in the family for generations can change. Healing from experiences of abuse and/or neglect can take place as we find our voice, ask for what we want, and treat ourselves with respect—and expect respect to be shown by others. If we had an overly controlling parent, we can learn how to share power through collaborative decision-making. We learn to trust that we will no longer allow ourselves to be dominated. If we had an absent parent lost through death, desertion, mental illness, or addiction, we can learn to negotiate for our needs.

If we had a parent who violated our personal boundaries, we can learn to tune into our inner alarms and find our voice to affirm them. If we grew up in a chaotic, unpredictable environment, we can co-create with our partner a harmonious, predictable living situation that provides a sense of safety. If we grew up in a rigid, overly constrained environment in which we felt the pressure of constantly having to live up to others' expectations, we can co-create a relationship that is characterized by spaciousness and creativity.

In becoming more cognizant of the wounds we may have experienced earlier in life, we become aware of what our work is and of how much we want to experience freedom from the limiting and now outmoded defensive patterns from childhood that are playing out in our life.

As we detach from our defenses, we become more aware of the feelings underlying them. The tender areas that we are attempting to heal—the old, painful memories of being violated, left, and misunderstood—surface, as do the ways that we have abandoned our authentic self in an attempt to be loved.

Only when we are able to acknowledge to ourselves the truth about our past do we become eligible to reap the bountiful harvest available through the creation of loving partnerships. The willingness to hold this vision as a genuine possibility is the basis of our commitment to doing our work. Much is required to fulfill that intention, but there is more within us than most of us realize. Much more.

101.

The payoffs

I f you've read, and hopefully implemented, some of the insights and guidelines we've included in the previous chapters of this book, you can probably more fully appreciate why you've heard so many people say, "Great relationships take a lot of *work*." And hopefully you've also heard that "it's a labor of love." Literally!

When you take on a challenge in which you are motivated by love rather than fear, the experience of doing the work is empowering rather than exhausting. Yet it's not just the way you feel during the process that shifts when you labor for love; mastering the art of conscious combat requires developing practices that result in quality-of-life changes extending far beyond an improvement in the ability to manage differences. They impact nearly every aspect of your life.

In this, our final chapter, we want to identify the results of the work we have previously alluded to and highlight the benefits you have to look forward to as you continue to integrate these practices into your life. Make no mistake; there will be moments when you feel doubt, discouragement, or disappointment—in yourself and/ or another person. This is only natural. Old, reinforced behavioral patterns don't dissolve immediately. Breaking habits that have become obsolete requires more repetition than you think it should, even when you understand that they no longer serve you. It takes time for the momentum that has been driving them to diminish and eventually end. But in the process, noticeable changes in your life will reinforce your commitment to self-development.

So, what benefits can you expect? Here are a few of them:

- A sense of belonging and connection
- Deepened feelings of self-trust, self-confidence, and self-esteem
- Alignment and harmony
- Greater enthusiasm and passion
- Unconditional mutual trust and trustworthiness
- Greater willingness to take interpersonal risks
- Creativity
- Skillful crisis management
- Bringing out the best in each other
- Deeper understanding and respect for each other's beliefs, needs, and values
- Greater collaborative and cooperative competence
- Reduced stress and anxiety
- Transformation of vision into reality
- An increase in wealth
- Greater fulfillment in the experience of sexual and emotional intimacy
- Giving and receiving inspiration
- Seeing previously unrecognized possibilities
- Feeling valued and appreciated
- Ever-deepening feelings of goodwill
- Enhanced listening skills
- Better health
- Extended longevity and enhanced quality of life
- Feeling loved and accepted for who you are
- Expanded capacity for compassion and empathy
- A sense of abundance and generosity
- A strengthening of the intention to be fully present
- Embodying a spirit of gratitude
- Greater clarity in regard to your life purpose
- More pleasure, ease, joy, and fun!

This list might seem grandiose or downright impossible, but we assure you that it's not. Abundant evidence from a great many people with whom we've worked over the years validates this claim. And we can personally attest to its veracity from our own experience in our fifty-plus years of being in a committed partnership. We've come a long way since our initial meeting in 1968. To say that we both had lot to learn (and to unlearn!) would be an understatement of massive proportions. We know that if we can do it, so can you! But don't take our word for it. Go for the gold!

Acknowledgments

With deepest gratitude to all who have inspired and supported us over the years in discovering what great relationships require, by modeling them in your lives and with us.

Special thanks to Stephen and Ondrea Levine, Harville Hendrix and Helen LaKelly Hunt, Gay and Kathlyn Hendrix, Sylvia and Seymour Boorstein, and John and Julie Gottman for exemplifying what truly fulfilling relationships can look like and illuminating the practices that create them.

Thanks also to our friends and colleagues who provided us the support that enabled us to accept the challenge of writing this book, particularly Susan Campbell, Melanie Joy, Gregg Levoy, and Marcia Naomi Berger. And to Thich Nhat Hanh and Jack Kornfield for their spiritual guidance. Thanks also go to our assistants Tiffanie Luna, Ellen Ferguson, and Sallie Iverson for your ongoing administrative help, without which this project would never have been completed.

And to Linda's women's group, Mary Amrita Arden, Lynn Gallo, Robert Valdez, Carolyn Levering, and Kim Karkos, and to Charlie's men's group, Doug Abrams, Gordon Wheeler, Mark Nicolson, Rich Sonnenblick, and Ben Saltzman, for your ongoing support and encouragement.

We are particularly grateful to our clients, students, and readers who shared their inspiring and courageous stories out of a desire to contribute their lessons learned to others. They represent the heart of this book.

About the Authors

L inda Bloom, LCSW, and Charlie Bloom, MSW, are psychotherapists and marriage counselors who have presented seminars and workshops on communication and relationships throughout the country and internationally since 1986. They are co-authors of several books, including the best seller *101 Things I Wish I Knew When I Got Married: Simple Lessons to Make Love Last*, which has sold over 100,000 copies. Their books have been translated into several languages. They have been on the teaching faculty at the Esalen Institute, the Kripalu Center for Yoga and Health, the University of California, Berkeley Extension, JFK University, and the California Institute of Integral Studies. They provide educational and counseling services to individuals and couples, and are bloggers for several online journals, including *Psychology Today* where their posts have received over 10,000,000 hits since 2011.

Charlie and Linda have been married since 1972 and have two grown children and three growing grandsons. They live and practice in Santa Cruz, California. Their website is www.bloomwork.com, and they can be reached by phone (831-421-9822) or email (lcbloom@ bloomwork.com).

CPSIA information can be obtained
at www.ICGtesting.com
Printed in the USA
BVHW072213310123
657546BV00001B/14

9 781646 638109